Sweet Sicily

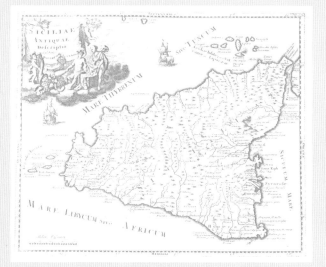

Sweet Sicily

The Story of an
Island and Her Pastries

Victoria Granof

Photographs by Linda V. Lewis,

Thomas Michael Alleman, and Melo Minnella

ReganBooks

An Imprint of HarperCollins*Publishers*

Opposite title page: Triumph of Gluttony, recipe on page 142

HarperCollins books may be purchased for educational, business, or sales promotional use.
For information please write: Special Markets Department, HarperCollins Publishers Inc.,
10 East 53rd Street, New York, NY 10022.

Color photographs by Linda V. Lewis; black-and-white photographs by Thomas Michael Alleman;
photographs on pages 22, 25, 28, 29, 30, and 43 by Melo Minnella. Photographs by Minnella appear
through his generosity and that of Bruno Leopardi, publisher of the magazine *Sicilia Ritrovata*,
to which Minnella is a frequent contributor.

FIRST EDITION

Design by Jessica Shatan

Library of Congress Cataloging-in-Publication Data
Granof, Victoria
Sweet Sicily : the story of an island and her pastries / Victoria Granof.—1st ed.
p. cm.
Includes bibliographical references and index.
ISBN 0-06-039323-8
1. Pastry. 2. Desserts 3. Cookery, Italian. I. Title

TX773 .G694 2001
641.8'65—dc21
00-045753

01 02 03 04 05 ❖/TP 10 9 8 7 6 5 4 3 2 1

To my nonna Victoria

and to her nonna Victoria

✳

Scorning the table of drinks, glittering with crystal and silver on the right, he moved left toward that of the sweetmeats. Huge blond babas, Mont Blancs snowy with whipped cream, cakes speckled with white almonds and green pistachio nuts, hillocks of chocolate-covered pastry, brown and rich as the topsoil of the Catanian plain from which, in fact, through many a twist and turn they had come, pink ices, champagne ices, coffee ices, all parfaits, which fell apart with a squelch as the knife cleft them, melody in major of crystallized cherries, acid notes of yellow pineapple, and those cakes called "triumphs of gluttony" filled with green pistachio paste, and shameless "virgin's cakes" shaped like breasts. Don Fabrizio asked for some of these and, as he held them in his plate, looked like a profane caricature of Saint Agatha. "Why ever didn't the Holy Office forbid these cakes when it had the chance? Saint Agatha's sliced-off breasts sold by convents, devoured at dances! Well!"

—Il Gattopardo *(The Leopard)*, GIUSEPPE TOMASI DI LAMPEDUSA

Contents

Introduction

There's nothing subtle about Sicily. She is the most captivating and misunderstood island in the world.

Far greater than those who malign her, Sicily is an island with thousands of years of fascinating—and vital—history. Fast, brash, and bewitching, she has the power to enchant you.

Sicily today is a collision of ancient and modern, at once reverent, superstitious, languorous, proud, naïve, artful, sensuous, dark, and passionate. She bears the weight of centuries of foreign domination—and nowhere more apparently than in her food. The Greeks, Romans, Normans, Austrians, French, Bourbons, and Saracens all took their turns with her, leaving behind legacies of flavor, color, and texture that would eventually find their way into her sweets, from the sherbets, ices, and floral essences of the Arabs to the cream cakes of the Spaniards.

More symbols of culture than mere sweets to eat, Sicilian pastries are imbued with religious, mystical, and historic significance. Every holiday is an opportunity to enjoy the myriad pastries prepared specifically for the occasion. Meticulously crafted marzipan lambs herald the approach of springtime, and luscious fig-and-spice-filled cakes signal the advent of Christmas. Pastries of devotion are prepared in convents, homes, and shops to honor the patron saints of Sicily's towns and regions.

Sugar makes Sicilians happy. It gets them through the day. During the steamy Sicilian summer, breakfast consists of a soft, faintly sweet bun filled with lemon or almond *gelato*. In every Sicilian town, no matter how humble, the evening *passeggiata,* the languorous, ritual stroll down the main street, always includes a stop at one of the many pastry shops for a *caffè* and something sweet. Sicilians wouldn't dream of paying a social visit without bringing along an exquisitely wrapped package of pastries from their local *pasticceria.*

I first learned about Sicily's pastries from a chef I worked with in an Italian restaurant in Los Angeles. I was just out of culinary school and she had spent the summer traveling throughout Italy. While we rolled out endless sheets of pastry

dough, she regaled me with stories of Italy and the foods she found there. When I learned that in Sicily they eat ice cream for *breakfast,* I knew I had to experience it for myself!

It took me ten years to get there, and in the meantime I read everything I could on Sicily and planned my trip meticulously. Still, nothing prepared me for the sensory bombardment that greeted me upon my arrival in Palermo, Sicily's capital. The airport smelled of coffee, aftershave, and sweat. People everywhere were screaming and gesturing at each other, kissing and crying and smoking, all at the same time. A whole planeful of baggage was lost, so officials passed out cookies!

I was in love.

Shortly after my return to the United States, I happened to read an article about Maria Grammatico, a pastry chef in Sicily. This formidable woman had spent her childhood living in a convent in the medieval town of Erice, where the nuns taught

her the ancient art of pastry making. Now she ran a pastry shop of her own in the same town. As a pastry chef myself, I was intrigued by her story. And saddened. She lamented the fact that few young people wanted to learn the art nowadays, and she feared it would soon be lost.

Although I received formal training as a pastry chef, the most precious culinary knowledge I possess is what I learned from my *nonna* (grandmother), who learned it from her *nonna*. I sympathized wholeheartedly with Signora Grammatico's plight.

That's when I knew I had to write this book.

✸

During subsequent visits to Sicily, I have poked around this magical island, visiting pastry shops, convents, restaurants, street markets, and private homes, learning to prepare—and eating—more sweets than I ever thought possible. I have gone with no agenda other than to explore Sicily and learn about her pastries, allowing her to lead me where she wanted me to go. Each time I have come home enriched by more discoveries and friendships.

This book is a product of those sojourns, and a tribute to all the people who shared so generously of their traditions, their stories, and their recipes. These recipes are only a few out of the thousands that exist today. Although it was necessary to adapt them for use in American kitchens, I have taken great care to preserve their spirit.

It is my hope that you will find the opportunity to visit this remarkable island and experience her sweet treasures for yourself.

You'll be amazed at what you find there.

A Brief History of Sweet Sicily

"*T*wo thousand five hundred lire, *signorina*. And that's my best price. You understand, my honey comes from Siculan bees that drink the nectar of Greek flowers. Best in all the Hyblaea!"

I was driving west from Siracusa through the Hyblaean Mountains and had stopped to buy some honey. If it did come from Siculan bees, as this man was claiming, I was about to buy a jar of some very ancient history. Not that I doubted his claim. The Siculi made their home in this part of Sicily more than twenty-five hundred years ago. They are believed to have been among the first inhabitants of the island. The necropolis at Pantalica—eight thousand troglodyte tombs carved out of the sides of vertiginous cliffs—are the work of the Siculi. And that's where I was headed when I stopped for honey.

Opposite: Detail of a mosaic in Villa Romana di Casale, Piazza Armerina

To understand their history is to understand Sicilians. Their fierce pride comes from being lusted after and lorded over by almost every civilization on earth for more than two thousand years—and surviving.

Historical Time Line of Sicily

650 B.C.	*The Siculi, the Sicani, and the Elymi are the first known inhabitants of Sicily, during the Late Bronze Age.*
735 B.C.	*The first Greek settlement is established at Naxos.*
734 B.C.	*The colony of Siracusa is settled by Greeks from Corinth.*
	Honey, ricotta, hazelnuts, walnuts, grapes, figs, and pomegranates arrive with the Corinthians.
	The Greeks construct the hortus, or kitchen garden.
201 B.C.	*The Punic Wars give control of Sicily to the Roman Republic.*
	Exports of wheat and barley to Rome earn Sicily the nickname "Granary of Rome."
	Latifundia, *feudal landholdings, are formed.*
	Cherries, plums, and citron are imported from Asia.
491	*The Goths assume control of Sicily, uniting it with Italy to form the Ostrogoth Kingdom of Italy.*
535	*Sicily is annexed to the Byzantine Empire.*
827	*The Saracens land at Mazara del Vallo to begin their conquest of Sicily.*
902	*The Saracens plant sugarcane, citrus, rice, bananas, mulberries, date palms, pistachios, watermelon, and apricots. They figure out how to make ice cream.*
	Irrigation methods are instituted in Sicily. Agriculture flourishes.
1060	*The Norman conquest begins, led by brothers Roger and Robert Hauteville. The gene for blue eyes enters the Sicilian gene pool.*

1091	*All of Sicily and the Calabrian Peninsula on mainland Italy fall to Norman rule. Roger is declared Count Roger I of Sicily.*
1112	*Roger I is succeeded by his son, Roger II.*
1154	*William I (the Bad) succeeds his father, Roger II. He is despised.*
1166	*William II (the Good) inherits the throne from his father and designates his aunt Constance as his heir.*
1189	*Norman rule ends. Henry VI of Swabia claims the throne on behalf of his wife, Constance.*
1208	*Frederick II, son of Henry VI, ascends the throne. The gene for red hair enters the Sicilian gene pool.*
1268	*Swabian rule ends. Pope Clement IV invests Charles, Count of Anjou and Provence, with the crown of Sicily.*
1282	*A French soldier insults a Sicilian maiden on her way into church for Vesper services. Thus begins the popular uprising known as the Sicilian Vespers, leading to the eventual end of French rule.*
1302	*The Treaty of Caltabellota gives control of Sicily to Spain under King Peter of Aragon.*
1492	*The Spanish Inquisition forces the expulsion of Jews from Sicily. With the Jews goes Sicily's thriving sugar industry.*
	Chocolate, squash, tomatoes, peppers, and cactus are brought to Sicily from Mexico on Spanish ships.

1535	*Pastry making takes hold in the kitchens of convents and monasteries.*
1713	*Sicily is turned over to the Duke of Savoy in the Spanish War over Succession.*
1716	*Savoyard rule ends. The Treaty of the Hague gives control of Sicily to Austria.*
1734	*Charles V of Bourbon claims the throne on behalf of Spain.*
1767	*Ferdinand I, the son of Charles V, inherits the throne of Sicily. He rules with his wife, Maria Carolina, sister of Marie Antoinette, from their court at Naples.*
1805	*The Royal Court relocates to Palermo. French chefs arrive to cater to the needs of the court. The aristocracy eats well.*
	Swiss pastry chefs arrive in Sicily and set up shop in Palermo and Catania.
1816	*The Kingdoms of Naples and Sicily are united to form the Kingdom of the Two Sicilies. Corruption is at an all-time high.*
1860	*Sicily is liberated from Spanish rule by Giuseppe Garibaldi, who leads a populist overthrow of the corrupt Bourbon government.*
1861	*With the annexation of "The Two Sicilies," Sicily is unified with Italy.*

TAORMINA

Fontana del Duomo

CARTOLINA POSTALE ITALIANA
(CARTE POSTALE D'ITALIE.)

at this place they water also the donkeys, it is a grand old spot, and to us a conundrum how the boys like the women beside those jugs when filled with water and when empty then dishwise, yesterday while passing a little girl was carrying on her head a tin cup filled, it is probably the way they learn the stunt early.

John Jaburg Jr.

April 21. 1906.

51474 4

Sicily's recorded history begins with the Greeks and Phoenicians in a land they called Trinacria, referring to her triangular shape. Her emblem was the head of Medusa, surrounded by three legs, representing the three extremities of the island—one pointed toward Africa, one toward Asia, and the other toward Europe. Such was her beauty and situation that the next two millennia would see conquerors from all these lands descending upon her shores to have their way with her.

Sicily's first suitors were the Greeks, who in 735 B.C. established a colony at Naxos on her east coast. The expedition was led by a sailor who had washed ashore in a shipwreck and returned to Greece with stories of rich pastures and fields redolent with flowering thyme.

The colony of Siracusa was founded in 734 B.C., and others followed soon after. To these rich but largely uncultivated lands, the colonists introduced olives, grapes, figs, pomegranates, wheat, walnuts, and hazelnuts. Siculan bees were already hard at work

making honey that the Greeks would require as offerings to their goddess Aphrodite. And there was certainly cheese. The rich pastures nourished sheep and goats whose milk was made into the cheese we know today as *ricotta.*

The history of sweets at this time is sketchy, but we do have writings from the period that speak of the *opsophagis,* greedy gatherings, where *dulcis in fundo,* sweets made of honey, nuts, milk, and flour, were served with baskets of fresh fruit and sweet wine at the end of a meal. Later, Romans would leave documentation of several desserts, still made today, that date back to the era of the Greeks.

They made a custard of *ricotta,* honey, and eggs called *tyropatinum*—a sweet version of the cheese pie known in today's Greece as *tyropita.* Ricotta was also mixed in equal parts with the fragrant thyme honey of the Hyblean Mountains to make what the Romans called *mel et caseum,* a preparation that, with the addition of candied citrus and chocolate bits, is a current favorite. And finally, honey cakes that the Greeks prepared as offerings to the goddess Aphrodite bear a strong resemblance to the *mostaccioli* made all over the island today.

The colonies continued to grow and prosper, particularly Siracusa, which eventually extended its domain over the whole southeastern corner of the island. Throughout the island, the settlers constructed *horti:* vegetable gardens fenced in with stone walls that were the predecessor of the kitchen gardens called *orti* found in present-day Sicily.

This rapid colonization worried the Phoenicians. The Greek colonies were threatening their trade routes through the Straits of Messina. It was inevitable that battles would ensue, but the Greeks temporarily kept the Phoenicians at bay with their victory at Himera in 480 B.C.

Thereafter followed the golden age of Greek Sicily, when Siracusa, which had become the greatest city in the world, defeated a powerful campaign waged against it by a jealous and intimidated Athens. This era saw the construction of magnificent temples, acknowledged today as the most prodigious examples of Greek architecture outside Greece itself.

Temple of Concord, Agrigento

Greek control of the island ended for the most part in the middle of the third century B.C., when the Romans, who had come to control all of southern Italy, appeared on the scene to threaten the trade routes of the Phoenicians. The Punic Wars gave control of Sicily to the Roman Republic in 201 B.C.

Under Republican rule, Sicily quickly lost much of the prosperity it had enjoyed. The immense feudal landholdings called *latifundia* were controlled by corrupt landlords and cultivated by slaves, leading to many an armed revolt followed by bloody repression. The proceeds from the *latifundia* paid for luxurious estates and playgrounds for the aristocracy, some of which became centers of art and recreation for the Roman *bon ton*. Villa Romana di Casale in Piazza Armerina, where the famous Bikini Girls are depicted among its more than 3,000 square feet of mosaic floors, was built around this time, supposedly as the summer getaway of Emperor Maximianus.

Then, under the Roman Empire, Sicily settled into a period of peaceful prosperity. Augustus and Hadrian were admired for their dedication to the development of agriculture. The gluttonous Roman general Lucullus imported cherries, plums, and citrons

from Asia Minor to keep company with the cardamom, ginger, cinnamon, nutmeg, and allspice in the Roman pantry.

It was at this time that Marcus Gabius Apicius—educator, gourmand, and bon vivant—wrote *De Re Coquinaria (Cookery and Dining in Imperial Rome),* a document

that meticulously recorded the eating and dining habits of the Roman Empire. A gastronomic zealot, Apicius was said to have spent a fortune on his appetite over a period of several years. When he realized that he could not afford to continue eating in the style to which he had become accustomed, he ended his life by ingesting poison at a banquet arranged just for the occasion.

Though Apicius' document is lengthy and informative, there is not much information on *dulcia* (confections), although the ancients were known to be experts on them. There is evidence at the Casa del Forno—a bakery in the excavations at Pompeii—that the arts of baking and confectionery were highly developed and specialized, much as they are today.

I love the fact that some of Apicius' recipes have survived almost unaltered to this day. The very first *biscotto* may be one listed as *aliter dulcia* (another sweet), and calls for making a dough of nuts, spices, honey, wine, flour, milk, and eggs, baking it once, cooling the dough, cutting it into "handy pieces like small cookies," and frying them. This was a specialty of the *crustularius,* or *biscotti* baker. The *dulciarius,* or cake baker, worked with honey, inspiring this quote from another Roman, Martial: "That hand will construct for you a thousand sweet figures of art; for it the frugal bee principally labors."

Desserts in Roman times were called *mensae secundae,* second meals, or *mensae pomorum,* fruit meals, consisting as they did of fruit or fruit-based sweets. Strict sumptuary laws and taxes governed their consumption, and fines were imposed for noncompliance. These laws were designed to safeguard the morals and health of the people, but in fact served to pad the Emperor's coffers and provide kickbacks to the civil health inspectors.

With the breakup of the Roman Empire, the Vandals of North Africa swooped down on Sicily and lay claim to her in 468. Right behind them arrived the Goths, who, from their base at present-day Hungary, took control of the island in 491. Thus Sicily was united with Italy for a short, peaceful interlude to form the Ostrogoth Kingdom of Italy. In 535 Emperor Justinian ordered the conquest of Sicily for annexation to the Eastern Byzantine Empire.

By the early eighth century the Saracens were beginning to make their presence known in this part of the world. Of mixed Berber and Arab blood, they occupied a new kingdom on the north coast of Africa, whence they could greedily eye their newest conquest. In 827 ten thousand Saracen troops landed at Mazara del Vallo on Sicily's west coast, establishing a foothold on the island. Slowly they overtook Palermo, Messina, and Enna, and with the fall of Siracusa in 878, total success was assured. One of the first things the Saracens did was to move the capital from Siracusa to Palermo, where it remains today. Even now, the western part of Sicily is casually referred to as "the Arab side," while the east is thought of as "the Greek side."

It would be difficult to exaggerate the contributions these people made to the Sicily we know today. Poetry and literature flowered in Palermo, the center of Arab-Sicilian life. The Arabs introduced new cash crops, including cotton, linen, rice, and sugarcane. Land was divided into small plots, and new irrigation channels aided the intensive farming.

Lush gardens of lemons, bitter orange, bananas, date palms, pistachios, mulberries, watermelon, apricots, and tangerines flourished in the *horti* left by the Greeks. Fragrant gardens of flowering jasmine, roses, and bergamot provided the flavoring for the exotic beverages the Arabs enjoyed, which they discovered could be mixed with the snow of Mount Etna to create ices, or *sharbat*. Go to any *gelateria* in Trapani, a city near the spot of the first invasion of 827, and you will find *scurzunera*, jasmine-scented ice. Jasmine and sometimes rose water are also used to scent *gelo di melone*, a watermelon pudding made in the western part of the island and eaten in July during the feast of Santa Rosalia, patroness of Palermo. The sesame candy known as *cubbaita* is virtually indistinguishable from that made in the Middle East today, but for the frequent addition of almonds.

There is a wonderful book called *Cucina Paradiso* by Clifford Wright that details the contributions of the Arabs to the cooking of Sicily today. His exhaustive research has led Wright to conclude that the two most famous desserts of Sicily, *cannoli* and

cassata, trace their roots back to the period of the Saracen occupation. The occupation lasted only two hundred years, but their influence on the art of pastry making remains strong to this day, due in great measure to the introduction of sugarcane, which formed the backbone of this culinary art.

✳

Although the Arabs and Berbers of Sicily were prosperous and sophisticated, dissension among them would eventually create a division of power, making way for the ensuing Norman conquest. Begun in 1060, it was led by brothers Roger and Robert Hauteville. These daring warriors fought their way south from their home base in present-day Normandy, France, until in 1091 all of Sicily and the Calabrian peninsula of southern Italy were under their control. With the blessing of the Pope, Roger I became the stern but beneficent Count Roger of Sicily, succeeded upon his death in 1112 by his son, Roger II. The second Roger crowned himself the first king of Sicily in Palermo Cathedral in 1130 and is the Roger best remembered in Sicily today.

These meat-and-potatoes men left the austerity of the north for a southern land bathed in sunshine and replete with all the virtues and vices of the east. In fact the many remnants of Arab culture in Sicily owe much to the Normans, who embraced their adopted culture fully while making few additions of their own.

King Roger II kept a harem and lived as a caliph. His court was multilingual, speaking French, Greek, and Arabic. He hired Arab chefs to prepare Arab food and hosted banquets of extraordinary luxury, served on plates of silver and gold. He retained Arab artisans to work alongside Norman architects and Byzantine mosaicists to create the dazzling Royal Palace in Palermo, with its golden mosaic Palatine Chapel.

Although to this day Sicily maintains the distinct imprints of Arab, Greek, and Byzantine rule, the Normans proved a unifying force among these civilizations. So it was that in one hundred years the Normans were responsible for establishing a singular culture of immense splendor.

Norman rule ended in 1189 when upon William's death, his aunt Constance inherited the throne, claimed on her behalf by her husband, Henry VI of Swabia (in present-day Germany). Upon Henry's death his son Frederick II took over the throne. Only fourteen at the time of his accession, Frederick became known as Stupor Mundi, Wonder of the World. This oddly intellectual ruler became a great statesman and legislator and was the first to pass laws regulating the confectioner's trade.

History is weak, however, on the subject of recorded recipes. In the Middle Ages, strict secrecy was employed by cooks, physicians, and alchemists regarding potentially lucrative formulas, all known as "Rx." Thus few, if any, recorded recipes survive from that time.

Chiesa Matrice, Erice

The end of Swabian rule came in 1268, when Pope Clement IV invested Charles, Count of Anjou and Provence, with the Crown of Sicily. It would be lovely to think of this as a time when cream puffs waltzed into the kitchens of Sicily, but French rule is remembered for only one thing: the ruthlessness with which the ruler conquered his new realm and subjugated its occupants. This led to the popular uprising known as the Sicilian Vespers, and the eventual and complete massacre of the French in Sicily.

The Sicilian Vespers was followed by a war of independence between the French and Sicilians, aided by a new king, Peter of Aragon, who had been invited by a parliament of Sicilian nobles to take over the throne. After a twenty-one-year fight, independence under an Aragonese king was secured with the Treaty of Caltabellota in 1302. Aragonese rule would continue in relative peace under several successive kings until 1412.

Sugar fortunes were made during the 1400s by the Jews, who managed its cultivation and exportation through the spice route from Damascus to Venice, through the Straits of Messina. The Spanish Inquisition came to Sicily in 1493, and with the expulsion of the Jews went the foundation of the sugar industry. Charles III lifted the ban on Jews in the 1700s, but few returned, and by that time the cultivation of sugar had declined to the point that most of what was used on the island was imported from the Near East.

The availability of sugar and its importance during this time is apparent, judging by the recipes recorded in *De honesta voluptate,* written in 1474 by Bartolomeo Platina and the first cookbook to be printed using Gutenberg's recently invented press. Sugar was just beginning to make its transition from spice (used to season savory as well as sweet dishes) to settle into a category of its own and begin the pastry-as-art movement.

The influx of Spanish nobility under the House of Aragon and the fortunes made from feudal holdings expanded the ranks of Sicilian aristocracy. These nouveaux riches developed a taste for the showy and ostentatious embellishments associated with this Baroque period and, to a large extent, with the Sicily of modern times.

By the early 1500s, *cucina baronale* had taken hold in the kitchens of the aristocracy. It was a bull market for the nobility, who could well afford to indulge their taste

for excess, importing costly ingredients from the Continent. Elaborate ices and jellies shared buffet space with cakes constructed from a base of the newly arrived sponge cake, *pan di Spagna*.

This is when chocolate found its way into the Sicilian pantry. The Spanish had occupied Mexico and were intrigued by the chocolate they found, bringing it back to Sicily. A legacy of the Aztecs, chocolate was enjoyed primarily as a drink, boiled with water and whipped to a froth using the wooden implement called a *molinillo*. The town of Modica in the southeast corner of Sicily became the center of chocolate production because it was densely populated by aristocrats who could afford the ancient—and very expensive—chocolate-making methods, which have remained unchanged to this day. The unofficial curator of the tradition is Franco Ruta, who, with his son Pierpaolo, handcrafts exquisite chocolates in his shop, the Antica Dolceria Bonajuto in Modica, using methods identical to those of five hundred years ago.

Ships from the New World brought squash, which could be candied and used to embellish pastries, and cactus. Cactus fruit, called prickly pear in America, is known as *fichi d'India,* or Indian figs, in Sicily, and is a favorite for eating raw after a meal.

By 1713 Sicily had become a pawn in the Spanish War over Succession and was turned over to the Duke of Savoy. There are some very rich chocolate tortes called *torte savoia* made in Sicily today. These, along with ladyfingers, or *savoiardi,* are thought to have been invented during the period of Savoyard rule—and seem to be all that distinguish its three-year reign.

The end of the War over Spanish Succession released Sicily from Spanish domination and plunked it into the lap of Austria, where it remained for the next sixteen years to stagnate under Austrian rule. The Austrians were so disliked by the Sicilians that when young Charles V of Bourbon, in present-day Spain, arrived in 1734 to claim the throne, he was welcomed by the Sicilians, who were glad to be rid of the Austrians and again have a king to call their own. Under Bourbon rule, all of southern Italy and Sicily were united, with Naples as the seat of government, to become the "Kingdom of the Two Sicilies." Naples was then called "Sicily this side of the Straits" and Sicily was known as "Sicily that side of the Straits."

By 1767 Ferdinand I had inherited the throne but, taking little interest in ruling, left the day-to-day workings of the kingdom to his wife, Maria Carolina. The snobbish Maria Carolina preferred the frivolity of court life at Naples, but twice during their reign the king and queen were forced by circumstances to travel to Sicily. The couple was accompanied on their first trip by Lord Nelson, who brought to Sicily a taste for *all'inglese.* The royal cooks adopted the English trifle, a confection of sponge cake, liqueur, custard, whipped cream, and candied fruit, dubbing it *zuppa inglese* (English soup).

Circumstances of the Napoleonic Wars forced the royal couple to relocate to Palermo in 1805, along with their entire court. This time the queen sent word to her sister, Marie Antoinette, that she simply must have French chefs to attend to her culinary needs in what she had come to regard as their exile. These chefs became known as *monzù*, a corruption of the word *monsieur*. Gradually the Sicilians and Neapolitans who had apprenticed under the French *monzù* took over the kitchens and continued to bear that prestigious title.

By this time Swiss *pâtissiers* had arrived to satisfy the fashionably Continental sweet tooth of the aristocracy in Palermo and Catania. It was they, rather than the French, who were responsible for bringing the cream puffs to the island.

Probably more than anywhere else, the wealthy convents and monasteries of Palermo and Catania have been responsible for preserving the traditions of Sicilian pastry making. The Benedictine monastery at Catania survives today, and so do the friars' honey-drenched rice fritters, *crespelle di riso*. Convents, though, rather than monasteries, embraced pastry making as their second vocation. In addition to the wealthy convents, there existed throughout Sicily many others where unwed mothers, prostitutes, and other angels fallen from grace found solace in the warmth of the pastry kitchen.

In the early days of the convents, pastries were made as gifts for the nuns' confessor (the wealthier nuns had their own personal confessor), patrons, and visiting nobility. It wasn't until after the unification of Italy in 1860 that the sisters began selling their sweets. Church property, which amounted to one-tenth of all the land in Sicily, had been confiscated, and many convents closed. Others resorted to the selling of pastries to remain afloat.

In Mary Taylor Simeti's book *On Persephone's Island,* she speaks of a convent in Palermo where she purchased a spectacular bunch of grapes made entirely by hand of almond paste and fruit preserves. Following her lead, I arrived at what is now an upholstery shop in Piazza Venezia to be told by two elderly ladies that the convent had recently closed and the remaining "very ancient" nuns were living out their retirement at a neighboring facility. I consoled myself at the Abbey of Santo Spirito in Agrigento, where the sisters are not nearly as ancient and still create magnificent pastries.

Spanish rule ended in 1860 when Garibaldi's "thousand Redshirts" entered Sicily by sea from Lombardy in the north of Italy to lead a populist overthrow of the corrupt Bourbon government. Naples fell five months later, and the unification of Italy was achieved.

Sicilian pastries as we know them have gone through precious few changes in the past hundred years. Thankfully, the long arm of American fast food has not infiltrated Sicily's kitchens. In recent years, there has been a trend toward more healthful eating habits, but pastries seem to be exempt from this movement. I did find one enterprising young *gelataio,* at his cart on a Trapani sidewalk, hawking "*granita di limone— senza zucchero!*" (sugar-free). It was nothing more than a mouthful of painfully sour, frozen lemon juice. Apparently, he had not bothered to substitute another sweetener for the sugar!

I can't imagine staying away from sugar while in Sicily, but if you're determined, pay a visit to the Antico Chiosco at Mondello Beach in Palermo. They make a very acceptable sugar-free *gelato*—but for my money, I'd go for a really big slice of cold Sicilian watermelon.

Sicilian pastry chefs work passionately and with dogged determination to preserve their art. They stubbornly refuse to use anything other than strictly Sicilian ingredients or to stray from the recipes they have inherited.

Corrado Assenza, a pastry chef from the old Baroque city of Noto, is no exception. Signor Assenza and his brother Carlo begin work before sunrise, traipsing through orchard and field in search of plump almonds and jewel-like strawberries. They can and do tell you exactly which mountains the sheep that provide their ricotta grazed on and which orchards supply their pistachios. The Assenzas say that as long as the produce they use is grown on Sicilian soil, their history is preserved. You would therefore not figure these two for chefs who take liberties with the old recipes in order to conform to changing tastes. But they do, to delicious effect, and are quick to explain why: The art of pastry making is a living tradition—alive, they believe, only when it is used. In order for the tradition to survive it must be a part of everyday life and therefore relate to the way people live today. Where the Assenzas modify a recipe, it is so that its spirit may be preserved, allowing this tradition to live on—and more than two thousand years of history to continue.

Festive Sicily

*N*owhere else in the world is time marked with such vivid displays of pageantry and ceremony as in Sicily. From the solemnity of Christmas to the debauchery of Carnival, feast days, weddings, and harvests are celebrated with lush extravagance in even the tiniest of villages. Sicily's pagan roots lie just beneath the surface of its Catholicism, and festivals to honor the saints and the Madonna seem strangely similar to those rites performed in honor of Aphrodite, Demeter, and Persephone before the advent of Christianity.

Food carries profound symbolism to Sicilians, and every holiday, every festival, every rite of passage, has its traditional foods. They may take the form of an orange at Epiphany for prosperity, a marzipan lamb at Easter for rebirth, a pomegranate for fertility, or one of dozens of pastries and breads created to honor the occasion—the importance is in the tradition, year after year, keeping alive a people, its religion, and its culture.

Opposite: Holy Thursday procession, Marsala

The Sicilian Festival Year

Following are the primary holidays celebrated throughout Sicily. The towns listed after each one hold festivals every year to celebrate the holiday.

January

1 *Capodanno* (New Year's Day)
All over Sicily

First Saturday *Festa di Sant'Elia* and *Sagra della Ricotta* (Feast of Saint Elia and Ricotta Feast)
Nardo

6 *Epifania* (Epiphany)
Piana degli Albanesi, Mezzojuso

17 *Festa di Sant'Antonio Abate* (Feast of Saint Anthony Abate)
Nicolosi

20 *Festa di San Sebastiano* (Feast of Saint Sebastian)
Acireale

February

3–10 *Festa dei Mandorli in Fiore* (Almond Blossom Festival)
Agrigento

3–5 *Festa di Sant'Agata* (Feast of Saint Agatha)
Catania

40–45 days before Easter *Carnevale* (Carnival)
Sciacca, Termini Imerese, Piana degli Albanesi, Acireale

March

19 *Festa di San Giuseppe* (Feast of Saint Joseph)
Salemi, Santa Croce Camerina, Modica, Scicli

April

Settimana Santa (Holy Week)
All over Sicily

Domenica delle Palme (Palm Sunday)
Gangi, Butera, Caltabellota, Leonforte, Monterosso Almo

Martedì Santo (Holy Tuesday)
Scicli

Mercoledì Santo (Holy Wednesday)
San Fratello

Giovedì Santo (Holy Thursday)
San Fratello, Marsala, Caltanisetta, Lacena, Villalba

Venerdì Santo (Good Friday)
San Fratello, Enna, Trapani, Pietraperzia, Mezzojuso, Caltagirone, Chiaromonte Gulfo

Sabato Santo (Holy Saturday)
Caltagirone, Chiaromonte Gulfo, Villalba

Pasqua (Easter Sunday)
Enna, Caltagirone, Piana degli Albanesi, Prizzi, Terrasini, San Cataldo, Modica, Ispica, Scicli, San Biagio Platani

Holy Thursday in Villalba

Pasquetta (Easter Monday, a national holiday celebrated by picnics in the country)

All over Sicily

Last weekend *Sagra della Ricotta* (Ricotta Festival)

Buscemi

May

First Sunday *Festa di Santa Lucia* (Feast of Saint Lucy)

Siracusa

2 *Festa di San Sebastiano* (Feast of Saint Sebastian)

Melilli

8 *Festa di Sant'Alfio* (Feast of Saint Alfio)

Trecastagni

Third Sunday *Infiorata*

Noto

Sunday after the fortieth day following Easter *Festa dell'Ascensione* (Ascension Day)

Vita

June

First Sunday *Corpus Domini* (Corpus Christi)

Taormina, Caltagirone

3 *Festa della Madonna della Lettera* (Feast of the Madonna of the Letter)

Messina

13 *Festa di Sant'Antonio da Padova* (Feast of Saint Anthony of Padua)

Patti

Festive Sicily

25

24 *Festa dei Muzzuni* (Feast of the Urns)
Alcara li Fusi

24 *Festa di San Giovanni* (Feast of Saint John)
Aci Trezza

28–29 *Festa di San Pietro* (Feast of Saint Peter)
Palazzolo Acreide

29 *Festa di San Pietro* (Feast of Saint Peter)
Modica

July

First Sunday to second Sunday *Festa di San Calogero* (Feast of Saint Calogero)
Agrigento

First Saturday, Sunday, and Monday *Festa di Sant'Antonio Abate* (Feast of Saint Anthony Abate)
Nicolosi

11–15 *Festino di Santa Rosalia* (Feast of Saint Rosalia)
Palermo

17 *Festa della Maria Santissima di Porto Salvo* (Feast of Saint Mary)
Lipari

24–25 *Festa di San Giacomo* (Feast of Saint Giacomo)
Caltagirone

Last Sunday *Festa di Santa Febronia* (Feast of Saint Febronia)
Patti

August

Sometime in August *Sagra del Miele* (Feast of Honey)
Zafferana Etnea

13–14 *Processione dei Giganti* (Procession of the Giants)
Messina

14 *Palio dei Normanni* (Joust of the Normans)
Piazza Armerina

15 *Ferragosto* (August Holiday)

15 *Festa di Santa Venera* (Feast of Saint Venera)
Avola

19–21 *Festa di Santa Maria Santissima del Soccorso* (Feast of Saint Mary)
Castellamare del Golfo

Last Sunday *Sagra del Gelato* (Feast of Ice Cream)
Canicatti

August or September *Vendemmia* (Grape harvest and crush)

September

4 *Il Pellegrinaggio al Santuario di Santa Rosalia* (Pilgrimage to the Shrine of Santa Rosalia)
Palermo

8 *La Nascita della Vergine* (Birth of the Virgin)
Tindari

26–27 *Festa dei Santi Cosimo e Damiano* (Feast of Saints Cosimo and Damian)
Palermo

Second Sunday *Festa della Madonna a Mare* (Feast of the Madonna of the Sea)
Patti

October

First weekend *Sagra del Miele* (Feast of Honey)
Siracusa

First weekend *Sagra dei Pistacchi* (Feast of Pistachios)
Bronte

Second Sunday *Sagra della Mostarda e dei Fichi d'India* (Feast of Mostarda and Prickly Pears)
Militello

November

1 *Ognissanti* (All Saints' Day)
Palermo

2 *Festa dei Morti* (All Souls' Day)
All over Sicily

11 *Festa di San Martino* (Feast of Saint Martin)
Monreale, Floridia

December

4 *Festa di Santa Barbara* (Feast of Saint Barbara)
Paterno

12 *Festa della Santuzza* (Feast of Saint Lucy)
Siracusa

24 *Vigilia di Natale* (Christmas Eve)
Castelmola and all over Sicily

25 *Natale* (Christmas Day)
Presepio, Acireale

26 *Festa di Santo Stefano* (Feast of Saint Stephen)
Custonaci

31 *Capodanno* (New Year's Eve)
Palermo, Catania

Religious Festivals

Easter
La Pasqua

The Sicilian festival year reaches a crescendo during *Settimana Santa*, or Holy Week. It begins with Palm Sunday, when palm fronds are woven into intricate patterns and taken to the church to be blessed. The ceremonies climax on Easter Sunday, the day of resurrection and life that signals a new beginning for the people of Sicily.

Pastries and sweets prepared during the Easter season hold profound symbolism for Sicilians. Marzipan lambs are sold in pastry shops all over the island, come in all sizes, and are depicted either grazing or dozing in a pasture of candy grass adorned with a red flag. The red symbolizes the resurrection, and no proper lamb would be caught without one. Rendered in hard sugar, the paschal lamb becomes a *pupa di zucchero*, or sugar doll, like the ones that are made in November for All Souls' Day. In Marsala, the town's youngest children lead the Holy Thursday procession of the *Misteri Viventi*, or Living Mysteries, wearing colorfully embroidered robes and golden headpieces and bearing tiny marzipan lambs to signify regeneration. It is a custom in some towns for a young man to present one of these lambs as a gift to his fiancée, who returns the gesture with a marzipan heart. In Sicily, Easter is the time for reconciliation; for ending grudges, forgiving affronts, and making peace with one's neighbors. Thus the heart has become an important symbol of the season.

The procession of the Mysteries, or *I Misteri*, is one of the most dramatic of the hundreds that take place during Holy Week in Sicily. It begins in the afternoon of Good Friday and continues through the following day, and is a starkly moving depiction of the mysteries of Christ's passion.

Beginning on Palm Sunday and continuing to Easter Sunday, all of Sicily participates in these ancient celebrations of life, death, and rebirth. Pastries often play a part. At San Biagio

Platani, *Gli Archi di Pasqua,* the Arches of Easter, are enormous temporary arches that span the streets surrounding the cathedral. It is the faithful of the town who undertake the daunting task of decorating the arches in time for Easter Sunday. Hundreds of people labor lovingly to create thousands of loaves of hard, sweetened flatbread in symbolic shapes, that will adorn the arches, in addition to citrus fruits, rosemary, flowers, palm fronds, and date branches. The breads are called by various names depending on the town, but in general are known as *pupi cu l'ova,* or babies with an egg. The egg, like the lamb, symbolizes rebirth. Common shapes are doves, birds, hearts, baskets, candelabra, and snails (I have even seen what look like Donald Duck and Spider-Man).

Above: I Misteri, *Trapani*

Throughout Christendom, the dove is associated with Easter. According to Christian symbology, it represents the Annunciation, but in agrarian Sicily, it is also beloved for the return of vegetation it heralds, signaled by the olive branch it bears. Pastries made in its image are called *palummeddi,* or little doves.

The Festival of the Patron Saint
La Festa Patronale

I have met a lot of Lucias in Siracusa. Named after the patron saint of their hometown, all those Lucias (and, of course, the rest of the town) are bound by faith to pay homage to their protectress on December 12, and again in May, at the *festa patronale.* Santa Lucia's intercession on behalf of the people of Siracusa saved the city twice from famine—once by sending shiploads of grain (in December), and the other by sending a flock of doves (some say quail) in May. And that's a saint's job: to perform miracles. A patron saint is one who runs interference with the Almighty on a city's behalf, saving it from the scourges of famine, drought, and plague. Every Sicilian city, town, and village has a patron saint, and every patron saint is given a *festino* on his or her day.

For the believer, divine intervention carries with it the obligation of prayer, votive offering, and pilgrimage to receive grace, or give gratitude for grace received. It is interesting to note that this rite, though veiled in Christianity, has its roots in ancient Greek and Latin myth, with the worship of deities who had the power to descend from heaven and come to the aid of mortals. Ancient Sicilians lit bonfires, sacrificed animals, and led decorated carts through the streets in honor of Aphrodite, Demeter, Dionysius, and Persephone.

Even if the only animal to be sacrificed these days is the Easter lamb, and fireworks have replaced bonfires, the main event at every *festino* is still the procession of the saint's image, on a cart festooned with flowers or on the shoulders of the grateful, through the streets of the town. In many towns, the procession follows a path from church to church that has been covered in an intricate carpet of flower petals with religious symbolism, and crocheted or lace bedspreads are hung from balconies along the route. The saint is accompanied by musical bands, religious leaders, city officials, schoolchildren in first-communion dress, members of trade guilds, church groups, and women's circles, chanting or reciting prayers for the saint and bearing beautifully embroidered silk standards and, often, candles.

The *festino* in Palermo to honor Santa Rosalia, who saved the city from the plague in 1624, is the most spectacular in all of Sicily. It lasts five days and nights and is attended by over a quarter million people every year. A silver urn that holds the bones of the saint (which some cynics believe to be those of a goat, not Rosalia's at

Shrine of Santa Rosalia, Palermo

all) is brought down from her shrine in a grotto high up on Monte San Pellegrino. The urn is placed on a fabulously adorned fifty-foot-long cart and carried in a mile-long procession through the streets, accompanied by the usual cast of believers as well as by Cuban dancers, African drummers, and religious choruses from all over the island. By the fifth day, the celebration reaches a feverish pitch, and it is capped off by an extravagant fireworks display in the Bay of Palermo.

Sicilian saints love sweets, so they are honored on their day with special pastries prepared just for the occasion. For the May *festino* for Santa Lucia, the faithful eat almond cookies in which are embedded tiny circles of candied orange peel, called *gli occhi di Santa Lucia,* or Saint Lucy's eyes (Santa Lucia is also the protectress of eyes), and for her *festino* in December, they eat a pudding made of whole kernels of wheat, called *cuccia,* to recall the grain that saved the city from famine. Catania's Sant'Agata was said to have sliced off her breasts in martyrdom, and although this did not save the city from anything, she is nevertheless honored with *minni di vergine,* or virgin's breasts, small round cherry-topped pastries that are sold in pairs, in the same way as Saint Lucy's eyes. And on March 19 all of Sicily celebrates the *festa di San Giuseppe,* or Saint Joseph's Day, with the puffy sweet fritters called *sfinci,* or *zeppole,* tiny spheres of fried dough rolled in granulated sugar.

All Saints' Day and All Souls' Day
Ognissanti e la Festa dei Morti

Ognissanti, on November 1, is All Saints' Day, followed by All Souls' Day (known as *La Festa dei Morti,* Day of the Dead) on November 2. This is a time for communion with the dead, and it is a joyous holiday rather than the somber one you might expect. Fairs are set up in towns all over Sicily, where *pupi di zucchero,* colorful sugar statues in images ranging from knights and paladins to Donald Duck and Spider-Man,

and *frutti di martorana*, realistic fruits made entirely of marzipan, are sold in stalls alongside cookies, toys, housewares, and undergarments. Children awake on November 2 to find baskets that contain *pupi*, *martorana*, and toys, left for them by their dearly departed. In the afternoon, the town cemeteries take on a party atmosphere when families come with armloads of flowers and picnics that are shared at the gravesites of their ancestors.

Christmas
Natale

Natale con i tuoi, Pasqua con chi vuoi
Christmas with your family, Easter with whomever you wish

You would think that with Sicily's love of the showy and splendid, Sicilians would pull out all the stops for Christmas. Can't you just see a roly-poly fiberglass *Babbo Natale*, Papa Christmas, grinning down at you from the top of a Byzantine cathedral or a crumbling Baroque palace? Never. *Natale* centers on the celebration of the Nativity and, as in most Catholic countries, the festival is mainly religious. It is the one occasion when Sicilians come together to eat and pray in close family circles with reverence for the birth of the Savior. Every Sicilian church has a *presepe*, life-sized figures carved of wood and painted with exquisite detail, all in attendance at the birth of Christ. Several years ago, master pastry chef Giuseppe Chemi created an entire *presepe* out of marzipan for his shop window at the Pasticceria Etna in Taormina. If you ask him, he'll show you the photograph.

The first Sicilian Christmas in recorded history took place in 336, after Emperor Constantine approved Christian worship in the Roman Empire, and the occasion was much the same up until the 1930s. That was when an ad campaign for Coca-Cola featuring a jolly ol' Santa Claus introduced him to Sicily. They called him *Babbo Natale*, and he has become a familiar figure during the season.

Secular Festivals

LE SAGRE

*S*agras are secular festivals, usually in celebration of a harvest or a particular food that is a specialty of the area. There are *sagras* in honor of honey, ricotta, *gelato*, prickly pears, pistachios, olives, and sausage. In late August or early September, the *vendemmia*, or grape harvest, is celebrated all over Sicily. Dating from the days of the Roman Empire, it was known then as the *vinalia*, and a female lamb was slaughtered as an offering to Jupiter, the god of abundance, just before the first grapes were picked. No animals lose their lives at today's *vendemmias*, but prayers are offered to the Virgin Mary before any grapes are picked.

In the shadow of the ancient Greek temples in Agrigento, the blossoming of thousands of almond trees heralds the arrival of springtime. The first week of February is set aside for the *Festa dei Mandorle in Fiore*, or Almond Blossom Festival, at which parades, fireworks, and almonds in every guise from pastries to wine are enjoyed by thousands of people

Almond wine at the Bar Turrisi

from all over the world. The almond tree was considered by the ancient Greeks to be a symbol of virility, and if you go to the Bar Turrisi in Castelmola, where the specialty is homemade almond wine, you will see this symbol very well represented in the eight thousand or so penises made of every imaginable material that decorate the tiny four-floor bar.

There are other springtime festivals, and festivals that make no attempt to hide their pagan origins. In Noto, hundreds of townspeople work on bended knee for days on end to create the *infiorata,* a carpet of flowers that covers the blocks-long incline from the cathedral in the center of town. Each year, a mythological, religious, or folkloric theme is chosen for the design. In Gangi, just before Assumption Day on August 15, girls dressed in flowing white robes as Ceres, goddess of the hearth, ride ox-driven carts through the town, passing out pomegranates (an ancient symbol of rebirth and fertility) to the crowd. In June, the people of Alcara li Fusi celebrate the *Festa dei Muzzuni. Muzzuni* are silk-draped urns that are carried in procession in a pagan rite that honors Demeter, Mother of the Earth and goddess of fertility.

Carnival

Carnevale

You won't find plastic Pulcinella masks and grappa-soaked tourists at any of Sicily's Carnival celebrations. For the ten to fourteen days leading up to *Martedì Grasso* (Fat Tuesday, or Mardi Gras), Sicilians take to the streets to join in lusty parades and open-air revelry as a last hurrah before the forty-day period of abstinence known as Lent.

The celebrations, although cloaked in Catholicism, reveal early pagan and agrarian roots, especially in the smaller mountain villages, where floats are crafted out of wooden carts and trimmed with sheaves of wheat, citrus fruits, and flowers. The biggest and most beautiful of the island's parades takes place in Acireale, the swanky resort town on Sicily's east coast. Like all Mardi Gras celebrations, it is loud, bawdy, and excessive and involves unholy amounts of food and drink. Unlike others, though, at Acireale the floats are bedecked with hundreds of kilos of locally grown oranges and lemons, and all colors of fragrant spring blossoms, making a feast for the senses that is uniquely Mediterranean.

The single most favored Carnival sweets are the crispy, sugar-dusted pastry ribbons called *chiacchiere,* found all over the island during the season.

It is often a very debauched crowd that piles into church the next day, Ash Wednesday, only too ready to make their forty-day-long vows of abstinence.

The Sicilian Wedding
Le Nozze

Weddings are a big deal in Sicily. It seems that one in every five shop windows bears the sign *"liste di nozze,"* wedding registry, and does a brisk business in wedding gifts. The silver platters and crystal bonbon dishes, tagged with the name of their donor, are displayed at every wedding reception in a room specified for this purpose. This practice is carried over from the days when the bride's dowry was laid out for inspection by the *scrivanu* (scribe), whose job it was to prepare the valuation of the dowry, *vaggiata della roba.*

The pomp and ceremony accompanying the rite of marriage has its roots in Roman times, and many customs survive to this day. Few Sicilian couples would think of getting married in May or August, the months during which ancient Romans commemorated their dead. *"Donna a maggio sposata è mala donna."* (The woman who marries in May is a bad woman indeed.) Marriages of those who swim against the tide are not expected to last through the following winter. Likewise, Tuesday and Friday are considered unlucky days. Tuesday, *martedì,* is dedicated to Mars, god of war, and Friday, *venerdì,* is dedicated to Venus, goddess of love, who apparently likes to have the day to herself.

There are many opinions as to the origin of *bomboniere,* the little tulle bags of sugared almonds distributed at weddings today. Sicilian newlyweds have been showered with nuts, seeds, grains, and sweets ever since the Greeks tossed honey candy to ensure a sweet outcome to their marriages. In the sixteenth century, the Spanish custom of breaking a sweet biscuit over the heads of the couple came into practice. By the eighteenth century, fertility (nuts and seeds) was combined with harmony (honey and sugar), and the two became one—sugar-coated chickpeas known as *scacciu.* From there it must have been a short hop to sugared almonds, known in America as Jordan almonds and in Sicily as *confetti.*

Today, *bomboniere* are distributed at all festivities, and the almonds sometimes take a backseat to other trinkets in the bundle, from crystal ashtrays to plastic swans. But no matter how elaborate the vehicle, the *confetti* are always there—white for weddings, pink or blue for baptisms, red for graduations.

The white wedding dress came into vogue only about a century ago, when Britain's Queen Victoria set an example the world soon followed. The Sicilians, who love a good virgin, embraced it as a symbol of purity. Up until then, wedding gowns were brightly colored, even red, a color believed to ward off the evil eye. Not willing to tempt the hand of fate, Sicilian brides still wear a little "something red" on their wedding day.

The wedding reception, in a rented hall or banquet room, has replaced the meal held at the home of the bride's parents and the *bonlivata*. After the wedding meal, all the celebrants would follow the newlyweds on foot to their new home. The couple entered the house accompanied by the groom's mother, who remained in attendance in an adjoining room while the couple consummated their marriage. All this while the guests made merry outside, singing and dancing to ensure a good result—at the very least potency, and at best, pregnancy. It was the mother-in-law's job to hang the bloodied bedsheets from the balcony the next day, a testament to the bride's virginity. Of the many customs to have survived the passage of time, this is the one that Sicilian brides are most thankful has not!

Baking by Heart

Un pizzico qua, un pizzico là. A pinch here, a dash there. Sicilians cook by instinct. No one is chained to a measuring cup. Yes, grams and liters are used in recipes, but these are the tools of the novice. One is expected to develop a feel for the ingredients, thereafter measuring them in handfuls and heaps. A *manciata* (handful) is larger than a *pugnietta* (fistful), but the actual amount, of course, varies depending on whose hands are doing the measuring.

When I traveled through Sicily to research this book, I was rarely given a written recipe. "You must watch me do this," I was always told. When a recipe was written down, it was sometimes so vague as to be comical. At one pastry shop in Messina, the baker thoughtfully presented me with handwritten instructions for baking *n'zuddi,* crunchy almond cookies flavored with orange. Neither almonds nor oranges were listed in the ingredients! When I asked him about this, the bemused baker replied, "Well, *of course* there are almonds and orange in the recipe—can't you taste them?" He went on to detail the amounts: "*Una mucchietta* (a little heap) of almonds." And the orange? "*Quanto basta.*" The ubiquitous *quanto basta* is my favorite measurement of all—*as much as is enough.* Enough for what? Enough for the dough to feel the way it should. And this, I was told, I would learn to judge accurately as I developed *mani sapienti*—knowledgeable hands.

There is so much talk in America of standardizing recipes, of being *accurate.* Sicilians are amused by the concept of accuracy. "On a dry day, your flour may want more water, and then what good are those measuring cups, *signorina*? They are made of metal and are not *sensitive.*"

Something to bear in mind is that unlike Americans, who are always trying new recipes, Sicilian cooks may make a handful of recipes in their lifetime—over and over and over. Passed hand-to-hand and rarely written down, these recipes live on in the mind of the recipient, whose job it is to keep the tradition alive.

No wonder the *manciata* is more important than the gram.

Un pizzico, a pinch, of salt is necessary to bring out the sweetness in pastries. But once I tasted a *biscotto* made by the dashing young son of a well-known pastry chef in Agrigento. Was it salty! The chef apologized, with a shrug of the shoulders. "What can I do, *signorina*? My son is obsessed with love for his *ragazza* (girlfriend). He is distracted from his ingredients."

Sicilians say a pregnant woman cannot make delicate pastries because her hands are too hot. Better for her to get busy with the bread dough, they advise.

Oven temperature is another subject with understood rules. An oven is *dolce,* between 250° and 300°F, used for baking some cookies and delicate pastries; *medio,* between 300° and 350°F, for small sweets and tarts of marmalade or ricotta; *caldo,* between 350° and 400°F, for yeast-raised and cream-filled pastries and crunchy cookies; or *molto caldo,* between 400° and 475°F, for puff pastries and fresh fruit tarts. Experienced cooks can judge the oven temperature by the *prova della mano,* or hand test, which is nothing more than putting one's hand in a preheated oven for a second or two. In the days before calibrated electric and gas ovens, less experienced cooks resorted to the *prova della carta,* the paper test. Here's how it works:

Heat your oven. Place a piece of wet parchment paper in the oven for five minutes. If it turns golden blond, the oven is *dolce.* If it turns golden, the oven is *medio.* Brown paper indicates a *caldo* oven, and dark brown (the color of chestnut shells) means it's *molto caldo.* If the paper burns, lower the temperature by opening the oven door and removing some wood(!).

Baking like that may be a lot to expect of someone who is simply trying a new recipe from this book. Don't worry about having sophisticated tools—your hands are the most important tool of all. All I ask is that you enjoy the process of baking and that you treat your ingredients, and yourself, with patience and respect. You are preserving a tradition. That, to my mind, is more important than how impressed your friends may be with what you've made. In any case, if you bake the Sicilian way—by heart—you will taste it in the food.

E questo è la verità. And that's the truth.

The Sicilian Pantry

La Dispensa

Almonds, Bitter Almonds
Mandorle

One of the most glorious sights in Sicily is the valley around Agrigento in spring, when the almond trees are full of billowy pink blossoms. Sicilian almonds grow near Agrigento and in Avola, on the eastern part of the island. They have a higher oil content than California almonds, especially those that have been sitting on the grocer's shelf for who knows how long. Always buy whole raw, unblanched almonds and chop or grind them yourself; once almonds are chopped or ground, they lose texture and moisture very quickly.

Bitter almonds, which grow with abandon in Sicily, are the source of the "almond flavor" that is familiar to Americans because they are used in extract. The nuts themselves are illegal in the United States due to their natural cyanide content. I have made adjustments to the recipes for this book using pure almond extract together with regular sweet almonds, which makes a suitable substitute for the bitter almonds. Your other choice is to use the kernels from inside apricot or peach pits, which come closest to the flavor of bitter almonds;

they can be purchased in Chinese groceries under the name "almond seeds." To use fresh peach or apricot kernels, release them from their shells using a nutcracker, then blanch them in boiling water for 3 minutes, drain them, and dry them on a baking sheet in a 300-degree oven for 10 to 15 minutes.

Butter, Margarine, and Lard
Burro, Margarina, e Strutto

Lard used to be the principal fat used in Sicilian pastries—it gives dough a smooth, creamy texture and when used for frying produces a crispy lightness that you don't get with oil. It doesn't taste a bit piggy. Health-conscious Sicilians are beginning to use margarine, which gives a texture similar to that of lard. Butter is the last choice, because it's more costly than margarine or lard and gives the pastries a heavier texture. Using half butter and half margarine provides the flavor of butter and the lightness of margarine. It's up to you. Just don't use vegetable shortening unless a recipe specifically calls for it; it will leave an unpleasant coating on your tongue.

Candied Citrus Peels
Scorzette Candite

These are so simple to make and so often used in Sicilian baking that it is worth making up a batch yourself (see page 193). They keep for several months if stored in an airtight container. Many Italian groceries carry good-quality candied peel, or you could ask an Italian bakery in your area to sell you some. Only as a last resort should you consider using the plastic tubs of candied fruit sold in supermarkets. They taste more of chemicals than fruit. If you must, then grate a bit of fresh orange zest into your mixture to make up for their lack of flavor. I would add 1 teaspoon freshly grated zest to each ¼ cup candied peel.

Flour
Farina

Most pastry cooks in Sicily use a silky, golden flour called 00 or *doppio zero,* which is milled from soft winter wheat. It gives doughs a buttery flavor and crunchy texture, and it absorbs less liquid than U.S. all-purpose flour. I tested almost all the recipes in this book using both 00 and American flour. Should you wish to use 00 when all-purpose flour is listed, use 2 tablespoons less per cup. In those recipes calling for all-purpose flour, use unbleached all-purpose flour. You can find 00 flour in many Italian and specialty groceries or through mail order (see Sources).

Honey
Miele

Two types of honey are common in Sicily, and they have been used in baking for at least twenty-five hundred years: mildly perfumed orange blossom honey, *miele di zagara,* and the more robust thyme honey, *miele di timo.* The production of *miele di zagara* is concentrated in the area around Mount Etna in a town called Zafferana Etnea. The Hyblaean Mountains near Siracusa are home to *miele di timo.* All Greek markets and many Middle Eastern groceries carry *miele di timo,* as it is still hugely popular in Greece. Orange blossom honey is readily available in the United States. Just buy the best-quality raw honey you can find.

Pistachios
Pistacchi

The pistachio is a temperamental fruit—yes, it *is* a fruit. In fact, the term *frutta secca,* dried fruit, refers to all fruits, including those of the nut trees. There are both male and female pistachio trees, which must be pollinated by hand and bear fruit only every other year (odd years are fruit-bearing years).

Pistachios grow in two areas of Sicily: Bronte, on the slopes of Mount Etna, and Favara, near Agrigento. In the fall, when newly harvested, the nuts are a brilliant emerald green, turning paler as the months go by. Few Sicilian pistachios are currently exported beyond mainland Italy, but pistachios from California, Iran, and India are readily available throughout the United States. They have a slightly lower oil content and paler color than the Sicilian pistachio but are an acceptable substitute. Always buy pistachios raw, and from a source that does a brisk business in pistachios so their freshness is assured. Italian, Indian, and Middle Eastern groceries are your best bet.

Potato Starch
Fecola di Patate

Different from potato flour, this silky starch is used in place of flour in nut tortes. Look for it in the kosher section of supermarkets or at health food stores. Do *not* use instant mashed potatoes!

Raisins
Uva Passa

In Sicily, raisins are often dried in bunches with their stems intact and sold that way in open-air markets. Two of the three most common types have no equal in the United States. These are the *sultanina*, sweet golden-hued raisins grown in Turkey and Sicily, and the *zibibbo*, chubby reddish raisins with a winy flavor grown on the island of Pantelleria. The *uvette* are tiny little raisins comparable to our dried currants, which actually come from the Corinth grape, brought to the island by the Greeks from Corinth.

The golden raisins sold in the United States are nothing more than dark raisins bleached in a sulfur dioxide bath. Occasionally I have found raisins made from Red Flame grapes in farmers' markets in Los Angeles and San Francisco, which are as close as you'll get to the *zibibbo*, unless you dry Red Flame grapes yourself in a food dehydrator. Leave the grapes on their stems and allow then to dry for 2 days, turning them every few hours until they are dehydrated but still moist.

Sea Salt
Sale Marino

A pinch of salt brings out the flavor of sweets. Sea salt, particularly Sicilian sea salt, has a purity of flavor unlike that of ordinary table salt. *Sale marino di Trapani,* which is collected from fifteen-hundred-year-old salt flats at Trapani on the west coast of Sicily, is now carried in many gourmet markets in the United States. Any sea salt should be used a bit more sparingly than table salt.

Sesame Seeds
Semi di Sesamo

Sesame seeds are used lavishly in Sicilian bread baking as well as in pastries. Toasting them lightly brings out their nutty flavor. The best way to buy sesame seeds is in bulk from a health food store or a Japanese grocery. They have twice the flavor at half the price of those in supermarkets. Store them in an airtight container in the freezer for up to a year; the oil they contain is highly volatile and becomes rancid quickly.

Spices
Le Spezie

Sicilians buy their spices whole and grind them as needed. You will be surprised at how far superior their flavor is when freshly ground, especially in the case of cinnamon and cloves. (Grind the entire clove, including the stem.) An inexpensive coffee grinder does the job nicely—just be sure to use it only for spices. Spices diminish in flavor after 6 months, so be sure to purchase them from a source with a high turnover. Store spices in a cool dark place in an airtight container.

Sweet Wines
Vini da Dessert

Every region in Sicily produces a sweet wine from locally grown grapes that is used to bind dough and flavor cakes and pastries. Among these are Malvasia on the Aeolian Islands, Marsala and Moscato di Pantelleria in the west, Moscato di Noto in the southeast, and Vino di Mandorla in the east. The sweet wine most widely available in the United States is Marsala, and it can be used in any of these recipes that call for sweet wine.

Vanilla
Vaniglia

Sicilian cooks use little packets of vanilla sugar to flavor their sweets. The recipes in this book call for vanilla extract, since this is the form most commonly used in the United States. Be sure to buy real vanilla extract—imitation vanilla is worthless. To make your own vanilla sugar, simply cut a vanilla bean lengthwise in half and bury it in 1 pound of superfine or confectioners' sugar in a sealed glass jar. Let the sugar sit for 1 month before using it. Replace the sugar as you use it; the vanilla bean will continue to flavor it for at least 3 months. Use 1 tablespoon vanilla sugar in place of 1 teaspoon vanilla extract and reduce the sugar in the recipe accordingly.

Basic Recipes

Ricette di Base

$\mathcal{B}$efore you pull out your mixing bowls and spoons, take a moment to look at the recipes in this chapter. They are the building blocks of Sicilian *pasticceria*. If you're like me, you dislike cookbooks where every recipe calls for making three others first, and then assembling them into the final grand creation. This is different. It's the Sicilian way. So read on and don't be discouraged. None of the recipes in this section are at all complicated or require special equipment, and many can be made in advance and frozen. And with just these few basics, you can create dozens of different pastries.

Pastry Cream
Crema Pasticciera

Crema *pasticciera* found its way into Sicilian pastry kitchens by way of the French chefs called *monzù* (a corruption of the word *monsieur*), who were brought to Sicily in the early nineteenth century to cater to the Continental tastes of the king and queen. Queen Maria Carolina was a sister of France's Marie Antoinette, and she was responsible for opening the first royal dairy in Sicily during her reign. The purely Sicilian touches of lemon and cinnamon distinguish *crema pasticciera* from its French cousin.

2 cups milk, divided

1 strip lemon zest

One 3-inch cinnamon stick, broken

3 tablespoons cornstarch

5 egg yolks

½ cup sugar

2 teaspoons vanilla

In a small saucepan over medium heat, bring 1¾ cups of the milk, the lemon zest, and cinnamon stick to a boil. Meanwhile, in a small cup, combine the remaining ¼ cup milk and the cornstarch, stirring to dissolve the cornstarch. Set aside.

In a medium mixing bowl, whisk together the yolks and sugar.

When the milk has come to a boil, slowly pour it through a strainer onto the beaten yolks–sugar mixture, whisking constantly. Return this mixture to the saucepan and whisk in the milk-cornstarch mixture. Over medium heat, bring to a boil again, whisking constantly, and continue whisking until the mixture thickens. Add the vanilla, remove from the heat, and scrape into a bowl. Cover the surface of the cream with plastic wrap to prevent it from forming a skin. Chill before using. (The cream keeps for up to 3 days, tightly covered and refrigerated.)

MAKES ABOUT 3 CUPS

A t the Pasticceria Conti Gallenti in Bronte, the superior local pistachios are used to make this pastry cream. It is used to fill the tiny *cannoli* and *bignè* (cream puffs) for which the shop is famous.

Pistachio Pastry Cream
Crema al Pistacchio

½ cup shelled raw pistachios

½ cup sugar, divided

3 tablespoons cornstarch

2 cups milk, divided

1 strip lemon zest

One 3-inch cinnamon stick, broken

5 large egg yolks

1 teaspoon vanilla

In a small bowl, pour boiling water over the pistachios and allow to sit for 3 minutes. Drain the pistachios and rub them in a cloth towel to remove the papery skins.

In a food processor with the steel blade, process the pistachios with ¼ cup of the sugar to a fine powder.

In a small bowl, whisk together the cornstarch and ¼ cup of the milk until smooth.

In a small saucepan over medium heat, bring the remaining 1¾ cups milk, the lemon zest, and cinnamon stick to a boil. Meanwhile, in a medium bowl, whisk together the yolks and the remaining ¼ cup sugar; add the pistachio mixture.

When the milk has come to a boil, slowly pour it through a strainer onto the yolks, whisking constantly while you pour. Return this to the saucepan and whisk in the cornstarch-milk mixture. Over medium-low heat, bring to the boil again, whisking constantly, and continue to whisk until the mixture thickens and coats a spoon. Add the vanilla, remove from the heat, and strain into a bowl. Cover the surface of the cream with plastic wrap to prevent it from forming a skin. Chill before using. The cream keeps for up to 3 days, tightly covered and refrigerated.

MAKES ABOUT 3 CUPS

Chocolate Pastry Cream
Crema di Cioccolata

In the sixteenth century, chocolate was brought to Sicily from Mexico by Spanish noblemen who settled in the town of Modica. In the nearby town of Noto, master *pasticciere* Corrado Costanzo makes this silky, rich custard as a filling for his *cannoli*.

> 2 cups milk, divided
>
> 4 ounces unsweetened chocolate, chopped
>
> One 3-inch cinnamon stick, broken
>
> 3 tablespoons cornstarch
>
> 5 egg yolks
>
> ½ cup plus 2 tablespoons sugar
>
> 2 teaspoons vanilla

In a small saucepan over medium heat, bring 1½ cups of the milk, the chocolate, and cinnamon stick to a boil, whisking to melt the chocolate. The mixture may look curdled; this is fine.

Meanwhile, in a small bowl, combine the remaining ½ cup milk and the cornstarch, stirring to dissolve the cornstarch. Set aside.

In a medium mixing bowl, whisk together the yolks and the sugar.

When the chocolate-milk mixture has come to a boil, remove the cinnamon stick and slowly pour the milk onto the yolk-sugar mixture, whisking constantly. Return this mixture to the saucepan and whisk in the milk-cornstarch mixture. Over medium heat, bring to a boil again, whisking all the while, and continue to whisk until the mixture thickens. Add the vanilla, remove from the heat, and scrape into a bowl. Cover the surface of the cream with plastic wrap to prevent it from forming a skin. Chill before using. The cream keeps for up to 3 days, tightly covered and refrigerated.

MAKES ABOUT 3 CUPS

Ricotta Cream
Crema di Ricotta

You can't make good *crema di ricotta* without good ricotta. The finest in Sicily is thought to be from Piana degli Albanesi, a tiny mountain town just south of Palermo. Pastry chef Gaetano di Noto leads the pack in *cannoli* production from his *laboratorio* at the Bar di Noto near the center of town.

1½ pounds (3 cups) Homemade Ricotta Cheese (page 128) or store-bought, drained (see page 128)

1½ cups powdered sugar

2 teaspoons vanilla

½ cup chopped Squash Preserves (zuccata; page 190) or Citron Preserves (conserva di cedro; page 189)

½ cup chopped Candied Orange Peel (scorzetta d'arancia candita; page 193), optional

¼ cup semisweet chocolate chips

In a food processor or blender, mix the ricotta, powdered sugar, and vanilla until smooth. Transfer to a bowl and stir in the candied fruit and chocolate. Cover and chill. The cream keeps, tightly covered and refrigerated, for up to 3 days.

MAKES ABOUT 4 CUPS

J ust when you thought Sicilian pastries couldn't get any fancier, this icing comes along to prove you wrong. Simple though it is, *glassa di zucchero* puts the finishing touch on hundreds of pastries, from "virgin's breasts" to marzipan engagement hearts.

Sugar Icing
Glassa di Zucchero

6 cups powdered sugar

½ cup water

½ teaspoon vanilla

In a small bowl, whisk together the sugar, water, and vanilla until smooth and lump-free. Store, tightly covered, until ready to use. The icing keeps for up to 1 week, tightly covered and refrigerated. Add a little water if necessary to improve the consistency.

MAKES ABOUT 3 CUPS

Recipes

☀

55

Chocolate Icing
Glassa di Cioccolato

T his icing is used to frost the clove-scented cookies called *tetu* and to decorate the tops of the Sicilian cream puffs known as *bignè*.

½ cup sugar

¾ cup water

2 ounces unsweetened chocolate, roughly chopped

5 cups powdered sugar

In a small heavy-bottomed saucepan over medium-high heat, bring the sugar and water to a boil, stirring to dissolve the sugar. Boil until reduced by half, about 7 minutes; remove from the heat.

Add the chocolate and whisk until the chocolate is melted. Transfer the mixture to a medium bowl and whisk in the powdered sugar, a little at a time, until the icing is smooth. The icing firms as it cools, but you can rewarm it over low heat for a few minutes to loosen it up. The icing keeps for up to 1 week, covered and refrigerated. Bring to room temperature before using, or reheat in a double boiler until it liquefies.

MAKES ABOUT 3 CUPS

Lemon Icing
Glassa di Limone

Sicilian housewives use a long and laborious method for making a lemon icing that they use to decorate simple cookies and cakes. Signora Teresa Bambù, a modern housewife of about eighty years, taught me this way to do it. Besides Signora Teresa's *biscotti all'uovo*, this icing works well on *taralli* (sweet pastry rings) and *bignè* (cream puffs).

    6 cups powdered sugar
    Grated zest of 2 lemons
    ½ cup water

In a small mixing bowl, whisk all the ingredients together until smooth. Cover until ready to use. The icing keeps for up to 2 days, tightly covered and refrigerated. Add a little more water if needed to improve the consistency.

MAKES ABOUT 3 CUPS

Sponge Cake
Pan di Spagna

Pan di Spagna translates as "bread of Spain." During the period of Spanish domination in the sixteenth century, an elaborate style of cooking came into vogue in Sicily, called *cucina baronale*. Almost invariably, the Baroque flourishes that adorned the pastries of this era, such as the "triumph of gluttony" and *cassata gelata*, rested on a humble foundation of *pan di Spagna*. This is my *nonna*'s recipe.

6 eggs, separated

¾ cup sugar, divided

1 tablespoon hot water

1 teaspoon vanilla

Grated zest of 1 lemon

1¼ cups cake flour (see Note)

½ teaspoon baking powder

¼ teaspoon salt

Preheat the oven to 350 degrees. Line the bottom of a 10 by 3-inch springform pan with waxed paper or baking parchment.

In a large bowl, with an electric mixer, whip the egg yolks with ½ cup of the sugar, the water, vanilla, and lemon zest until light yellow and tripled in volume. Sift the flour, baking powder, and salt directly onto the yolk mixture and gently fold in.

In a separate bowl, with clean beaters, whip the egg whites until soft peaks form. Whip in the remaining ¼ cup sugar, a tablespoon at a time, until stiff peaks form. Fold the whites gently but with authority into the yolk-flour mixture until no white streaks remain.

Spread the batter evenly in the prepared pan and bake for 35 to 40 minutes, or until the cake is golden brown and the top springs back when lightly touched. Set upside down on a cooling rack and cool completely before removing from the pan.

MAKES ONE 10-INCH CAKE

NOTE: If cake flour is unavailable, substitute I cup unbleached all-purpose flour and ½ cup cornstarch. Sift both the flour and cornstarch well before measuring.

T wenty-five hundred years ago, the Greeks arrived in Sicily to find almond trees flourishing in the valley near Agrigento. Each February in Agrigento their blossoming is celebrated with a week long festival that takes place near the Valley of the Temples. Nothing is more ubiquitous in Sicilian pastry than almonds, and for good reason. They have an incomparably rich texture and a flavor that is earthy and pure.

Almond Paste
Pasta di Mandorle

Almond paste is a base recipe for many of the cookies in this book, including chewy almond cookies *(fior di mandorla)* and Saint Lucy's eyes, but it makes a fine cookie in its own right. Just roll teaspoonfuls of dough into balls, place on a baking sheet, flatten slightly with your hand or the bottom of a drinking glass dipped in sugar, and bake in a preheated 350-degree oven for 30 to 35 minutes, or until nicely browned.

3⅓ cups blanched whole almonds

2 cups sugar

2 tablespoons honey

2 teaspoons vanilla

¼ teaspoon pure almond extract

2 eggs, beaten lightly to blend

1 teaspoon grated lemon zest

Pinch of salt

To make the almond paste using a food processor, in a processor fitted with the steel blade, grind the almonds and sugar together, in two batches, to a fine powder. Do not overprocess, or the almonds will become oily, making the resulting pastry heavy and greasy. Return all the almonds to the processor and, with the machine running, add the remaining ingredients. Continue to process until the paste comes together in a ball.

Or, to prepare the paste the traditional way, grind the almonds and sugar together through a hand-cranked meat grinder. This produces a light, aerated mixture with no danger of oiliness. Transfer to a mixing bowl, stir in the remaining ingredients, and knead with dampened hands until smooth.

In either case, immediately wrap the finished paste tightly in plastic wrap to prevent it from drying out. It keeps for up to 3 days, refrigerated.

MAKES ABOUT 2 POUNDS; ENOUGH FOR 2 TO 3 DOZEN COOKIES

On my first trip to Sicily, I was captivated by the marzipan confections I found at the Pasticceria Roberto in Taormina. I talked Roberto and his father into letting me infiltrate their *laboratorio* for the three days it would take to make their weekly batch of *pasta reale*. *Pasta reale,* or *marzapane* as it is sometimes called, is the paste from which all sorts of marzipan sweets are crafted, the most famous among them being *frutti di martorana,* lifelike fruits made entirely of marzipan. Beginning with the blanching, peeling, and grinding of almost a hundred pounds of almonds, Roberto and his father spent the better part of a day making the marzipan that would eventually become hundreds of exquisite *frutti di martorana.* With a food processor or coffee grinder, you can make it in a fraction of the time.

3 cups blanched whole almonds

1½ cups sugar

½ cup light corn syrup

2 tablespoons lemon juice

Using a food processor fitted with the steel blade, grind the almonds with ½ cup of the sugar to a fine powder.

In a medium saucepan over low heat, stir together the corn syrup, lemon juice, and the remaining 1 cup sugar and cook, stirring constantly, until the sugar is completely dissolved. Remove from the heat and stir in the almond-sugar mixture until the mixture comes together in a solid mass. If you have a marble slab, here's your chance to use it. Lightly oil the marble, or a baking sheet, turn the marzipan out onto it, and leave it to cool.

When the marzipan is cool enough to handle, knead it, on the marble or a clean work surface, until smooth and satiny. Wrap tightly in plastic wrap and use within 1 day.

MAKES ABOUT 1½ POUNDS; ENOUGH FOR 6 LIFE-SIZED LEMONS

Sweet Pastry Dough

Pasta Frolla

½ pound (2 sticks) unsalted butter or margarine, softened

¾ cup sugar

2 egg yolks

1 teaspoon grated lemon zest

¼ teaspoon salt

4¾ cups 00 flour or 5 cups unbleached all-purpose flour

In a large mixing bowl, cream the butter and sugar. Beat in the yolks one at a time, mixing well after each addition. Add the lemon zest, salt, and flour, stirring until a soft dough forms. Wrap tightly in plastic wrap and refrigerate for at least 2 hours before using. The dough keeps for up to 2 days, tightly wrapped and refrigerated, and can also be frozen for up to 3 months, wrapped in a double thickness of plastic wrap. Defrost in the refrigerator overnight before using.

MAKES ABOUT 2 POUNDS; ENOUGH FOR THREE 9-INCH TARTS OR 3 DOZEN 2-INCH PASTRIES

When the Saracens invaded Sicily in the ninth century, they planted gardens of jasmine and roses to satisfy their taste for the exotic. At the Pasticceria Colicchia in Trapani, near the site of the original Saracen invasion, *acqua di gelsomino* is used to make jasmine *gelato* (*scurzunera*). You can use jasmine water as they did in the harems, to sprinkle on your bedsheets. Jasmine is the Arab symbol of hospitality.

4 cups unsprayed night-blooming jasmine blossoms (see above)

5 cups distilled water

Place the jasmine blossoms in a large glass container and cover with the water. Make sure every blossom is submerged. You may need to put a small plate the size of the opening of the container on top to coax the blossoms underwater. Leave, loosely covered, in a cool place overnight, or for at least 12 hours, but no more than 16 (or they will begin to rot).

Strain the jasmine water into a glass bottle and seal tightly. Store in the refrigerator for up to 3 days.

MAKES ABOUT 5 CUPS

Cookies and Small Pastries

Biscotti e Dolcetti

𝓘 have yet to visit a Sicilian home that doesn't have a supply of homemade cookies on hand at all times. You never know when someone will drop in for a *caffè* or a glass of wine, so you have to be prepared.

On one of my trips to Sicily, I was traveling with three other people. Linda, who was taking some of the photographs for this book, had a cousin in Partanna whom she hadn't seen in thirty years, so we had decided to take a break from our *cannoli* research and visit him. When we phoned to say we were coming, Andrea told us to meet him at the *piazza* at six P.M. precisely.

Not yet having mastered the freeway system (the exit signs are located *after* the off-ramps), not to mention being slowed

Opposite: Dolcini di Erice, page 108

down by the dozens of *cannoli* we had amassed during our research, we got lost. So at a quarter to *nine*—precisely—we arrived to find the *piazza* crowded with townfolk, and Linda, of course, had no idea what her cousin looked like after thirty years.

Apparently, though, the *piazza* patrol had been alerted, because not only did the very first person we approached identify Linda immediately as "*la cugina americana*," but he escorted us personally to Andrea's home. We were all welcomed as family, homemade wine was uncorked, and a six-hour meal of homemade everything ensued. Just when we thought there was no more room for another bite, Zia Sarina, matriarch of the Cangemi clan, brought out a tray of cookies and a bottle of her son's sweet homemade wine.

"*Prendete questi, per il viaggio.*" (Take these, for the journey.)

The wine tasted of mellowness and warmth and the cookies tasted of a mother's love.

We departed at three A.M. with gifts of home-pressed olive oil and Zia Sarina's cookies. The journey wasn't so bad either. The ballast went overboard, and after a six-hour meal, even the freeway seemed to make sense!

Aunt Sarina's Biscotti

Biscotti di Zia Sarina

8 tablespoons (1 stick) unsalted butter, softened

½ cup sugar

1 egg

1 teaspoon vanilla

2 tablespoons Tangerine Liqueur (mandarinetto; page 199),
*   orange liqueur, or orange juice*

Pinch of salt

1¾ cups 00 flour or 2 cups unbleached all-purpose flour

½ cup blanched whole almonds

In a large mixing bowl, cream the butter and sugar until light. Beat in the egg, vanilla, liqueur, and salt and mix until well blended. Stir in the flour until the dough forms a ball, then stir in the almonds.

Turn the dough out onto a lightly floured surface and knead gently for a minute or two. Then divide the dough in half and form it into 2 logs, each 1½ inches thick by 10 inches long. Wrap in plastic wrap or waxed paper and chill until firm, about 2 hours.

Preheat the oven to 375 degrees.

With a very sharp knife, cut the logs into ½-inch slices and lay the cookies 2 inches apart on ungreased baking sheets. Bake for 25 to 30 minutes, or until golden brown. Cool on a rack.

MAKES ABOUT 3 DOZEN

Sesame Cookies
Biscotti Regina

So there I was at the All Souls' Day carnival in Palermo, rooting around in the huge displays of cookies for one of these. Suddenly a *biscotto regina* was thrust in my face, held there by a clawlike device duct-taped to a very long stick controlled like the strings of a marionette by the proprietor of the next booth over. The competition is fierce for these, but you'll find them all over. This is one cookie that has emigrated successfully from the old country.

8 tablespoons (1 stick) unsalted
  butter, softened

½ cup sugar

2 egg yolks

½ cup milk

Grated zest of 1 lemon

2¼ cups 00 flour or 2½ cups unbleached all-purpose flour

2 teaspoons baking powder

¾ cup sesame seeds

In a large bowl, beat the butter and sugar together just until combined. Beat in the yolks, milk, and zest. (The mixture will seem curdled; do not panic.) Sift the flour with the baking powder and stir into the butter mixture, mixing until the dough comes together in a ball. Cover and refrigerate for at least 1 hour or up to 1 day, to make the dough easier to handle.

Preheat the oven to 375 degrees. Grease two large baking sheets.

Place the sesame seeds in a fine-mesh strainer and rinse well. Shake the strainer to remove excess water and turn the seeds out onto a board or into a shallow pan.

Remove the dough from the refrigerator, divide it into 8 equal pieces, and shape each piece into a ball. Roll each ball under your palms on a very lightly floured board into a rope about 8 inches long. With a sharp knife, cut each rope into 4 pieces. Roll each piece in the sesame seeds and place 2 inches apart on a greased baking sheet.

Bake for 20 to 25 minutes, or until well browned. Let cool for 5 minutes before removing from the pans. Cool on a rack.

MAKES 32

Little Tea Cookies
Biscottini da Tè

Order a cappuccino at the Bar Saint Honoré in Taormina, and you'll be treated to a tiny plate of these melt-in-your-mouth tea cookies. It's worth seeking out 00 flour (see Sources) to give these the pleasing crumbly texture that makes them so irresistible.

5 tablespoons unsalted butter or margarine, softened

⅔ cup sugar

2 egg yolks

1 teaspoon vanilla

¼ teaspoon salt

3⅓ cups 00 flour or 3⅔ cups unbleached all-purpose flour

Preheat the oven to 350 degrees.

In a large mixing bowl, cream the butter or margarine and sugar until blended. Beat in the egg yolks, one at a time. Then add the vanilla and salt and continue to mix until smooth. Stir in the flour, a little at a time, until the dough comes together in a ball. Turn the dough out onto a lightly floured work surface and knead for a minute or two.

Pinch off a tablespoonful of dough at a time and roll out under your palms on a work surface to form a 4-inch-long rope. Bring the ends around to form a circle and cross them over each other, pressing ever so lightly, just to seal.

Place the cookies 2 inches apart on ungreased baking sheets and bake for 20 to 25 minutes, or until barely golden. Do not overbake or they will become crunchy, which is good for some cookies, but not these. Cool on a rack.

MAKES ABOUT 5 DOZEN

I n her precious time off from her self-appointed post as docent at the Church of Santo Spirito in Agrigento, Signora Teresa Bambù bakes these simple cookies as she has for over fifty years. Just in case someone drops by. The name *biscotti all'uovo* means they are rich with eggs, but it's their tart, lemony bite that best characterizes them.

12 tablespoons (1½ sticks) unsalted butter or margarine, softened

½ cup sugar

3 eggs

¼ cup milk

Grated zest and juice of 1 lemon

3½ cups unbleached all-purpose flour

1 tablespoon baking powder

2 teaspoons baking soda

¼ teaspoon salt

1 recipe Lemon Icing (glassa di limone; page 57)

Preheat the oven to 350 degrees. Grease two large baking sheets.

In a large mixing bowl, cream the butter or margarine and sugar until well blended (but not fluffy, or the cookies will retain too much air and then collapse). Beat in the eggs, milk, zest, and juice.

Sift together the flour, baking powder, baking soda, and salt into another large bowl. Add the butter mixture until a dough forms. It will be slightly sticky. Turn the dough out onto a lightly floured work surface and knead gently for a few minutes, incorporating only enough additional flour to prevent the dough from sticking to the surface.

Pinch off a tablespoon of dough at a time, roll between the palms of your hands into a smooth ball, and place the balls 3 inches apart on the greased baking sheet.

Bake for 10 to 12 minutes, or until golden brown. While the cookies are still warm, dip the tops in the lemon icing, then set on a rack over a sheet of waxed paper or a baking sheet, to catch drips, and let cool.

MAKES ABOUT 3 DOZEN

Cookies and Small Pastries

Crunchy Spice Cookies
Piparelli

Abstinence during Lent means that for the forty days preceding Easter, Catholics all over Sicily are supposed to eat *cucina magra* (literally, lean food). This means no meat, no fat, no eggs. Theoretically. Modern Catholics get to choose what they give up for Lent, and this is called *fare un fioretto,* or making a sacrifice. There is little indication that pastries and sweets are even *near* the top of the "to give up" list, other than the presence of *quaresimali* (see page 76), the general term for the category of austere cookies that appear in pastry shops during the spring. *Piparelli* are the Lenten cookies that the people of Messina like best. At the Pasticceria Vinci Domenico in Messina, *piparelli* are such a favorite that they're now made year-round.

4 tablespoons (½ stick) unsalted butter or margarine, softened

¼ cup packed dark brown sugar

1 cup orange blossom honey

2 egg whites (kept separate)

3 cups unbleached all-purpose flour

1½ teaspoons baking soda

¼ teaspoon salt

¾ teaspoon ground cloves

½ teaspoon freshly ground black pepper

3 tablespoons chopped Candied Orange Peel (scorzetta d'arancia candita; page 193)

1 cup unblanched whole almonds

Preheat the oven to 375 degrees. Grease a baking sheet.

In a large bowl, cream the butter or margarine with the brown sugar and honey. Add 1 of the egg whites and mix until evenly blended. Sift together the flour, baking soda, salt, and spices into another bowl and add the butter mixture, stirring until the dough is smooth and no longer sticky.

Turn the dough out onto a lightly floured work surface and knead in the orange peel and almonds until evenly dispersed. Divide the dough into 3 pieces and form each piece into a log that is 8 inches long by 2 inches thick. Place the logs 3 inches apart on the greased baking sheet. Beat the remaining egg white lightly and brush the tops of the logs with it.

Bake the logs for 20 to 25 minutes, or until firm to the touch. Remove from the oven and allow to cool for 10 minutes. Reduce the oven temperature to 325 degrees. Slice the logs ¼ inch thick and lay the cookies on the baking sheet. Return to the oven for another 15 to 20 minutes to dry them out. The cookies will become crisp as they cool, so don't overbake them. Cool on a rack.

MAKES ABOUT 7 DOZEN

Crunchy Orange-Almond Cookies

N'zuddi

In Messina, these cookies are enjoyed during the Feast of Messina's patron saint, the Madonna della Lettera, on June 3. Their slightly squared shape mimics the letter that the Madonna was said to have written to the people of Messina in 43 A.D., which she hand-carried from Jerusalem. Unfortunately, the letter was destroyed in a fire in 1253, and its contents unknown, but the cookies live on. In Messina, *pasticcieria* owner Domenico Vinci, his vivacious wife, Brigitta, and their nephew Giuseppe work round the clock starting on the first of June to produce enough *n'zuddi* to feed the faithful during the festival.

   2 cups blanched whole almonds, divided

   4 cups unbleached all-purpose flour

   ½ teaspoon baking soda

   ½ teaspoon baking powder

   12 tablespoons (1½ sticks) unsalted butter, softened

   1½ cups sugar

Sweet Sicily

1 egg

1 tablespoon grated orange zest

7 tablespoons orange juice

1 teaspoon vanilla

Pinch of salt

Preheat the oven to 375 degrees.

Spread the almonds on a baking sheet and toast for 15 minutes, or until deep golden brown. Let cool.

Set aside 36 almonds. Grind the remaining almonds to a coarse powder in a food processor or in small batches in a coffee grinder. Transfer to a medium mixing bowl and sift in the flour, baking soda, and baking powder.

In a large mixing bowl, with a wooden spoon, beat the butter and sugar until blended. Beat the egg, then beat in the orange zest, juice, vanilla, and salt. Stir in the flour-almond mixture.

Pinch off a tablespoonful of dough at a time, roll into a ball between the palms of your hands, and place 3 inches apart on greased baking sheets. Flatten the balls to ½ inch thick under your palms, then gently coax the edges inward to create a loose square shape. Press a whole almond into the center of each cookie.

Bake the cookies for 30 to 35 minutes, or until deep golden brown. Let cool for 5 minutes before removing from the pans, then cool on a rack. The cookies will become very crunchy as they cool.

MAKES ABOUT 3 DOZEN

Lenten Biscuits
Quaresimali

In northern Italy, these crunchy cookies are known as *cantucci*, but in Sicily, they are *quaresimali*, from *Quaresima*, meaning Lent. Wherever you find them, they are best dunked in a sweet wine. High above Taormina, in the town of Castelmola, is the Bar Turrisi, where they have been making the most sublime almond wine for over a century. These are the biscuits they serve with the wine.

2 cups unbleached all-purpose flour

1½ teaspoons baking powder

¼ teaspoon salt

¾ cup blanched whole almonds

3 eggs

¾ cup sugar

¼ cup sweet wine, such as Marsala

½ teaspoon grated orange zest

Preheat the oven to 375 degrees. Grease a baking sheet.

Sift the flour, baking powder, and salt into a large mixing bowl. Stir in the almonds. In a small bowl, beat together 2 of the eggs, the sugar, wine, and zest until well blended. Stir into the flour mixture and mix until a dough forms.

Turn the dough out onto a lightly floured work surface and knead it gently a few times to distribute the almonds evenly. Divide the dough into 3 pieces and shape each piece into a log that is 8 inches long by 1½ inches thick. Place the logs 3 inches apart on the greased baking sheet. Beat the remaining egg lightly and brush the tops of the logs with it.

Bake the logs for 25 to 30 minutes, or until nicely browned and firm to the touch. Remove from the oven and allow to cool for no more than 10 minutes—they will harden quickly. Reduce the oven temperature to 325 degrees.

With a very sharp knife, cut the logs into ¼-inch-thick slices and lay the slices on two baking sheets. Return the cookies to the oven and bake for another 15 to 20 minutes, or until dark golden brown. Cool on a rack.

MAKES ABOUT 7 DOZEN

T hese fancifully swirled and twirled cookies are traditionally made at Christmastime with the season's *vino cotto,* or cooked grape must syrup, but molasses works perfectly in its place. Of course, if you have *vino cotto,* use it instead. In either case, *spicchiteddi* closely resemble gingerbread cookies in both flavor and texture.

8 tablespoons (1 stick) unsalted butter or margarine

½ cup honey

½ cup molasses or Cooked Grape Must Syrup (vino cotto; page 202)

½ cup sugar

2 teaspoons grated lemon zest

2 teaspoons vanilla

4½ cups unbleached all-purpose flour

2 teaspoons baking soda

2 teaspoons cinnamon

¼ teaspoon salt

½ cup blanched whole almonds

Preheat the oven to 375 degrees. Grease two large baking sheets.

In a small saucepan, over medium heat, combine the butter or margarine, honey, molasses (or *vino cotto*), and sugar and heat until the butter or shortening melts. Add the lemon zest and vanilla, remove from the heat, and let cool to lukewarm.

Meanwhile, sift together the flour, soda, cinnamon, and salt. Add the dry ingredients to the cooled butter mixture and stir until the dough comes together in a ball; it will be soft. Turn out onto a lightly floured work surface and knead gently for a minute or two. Pinch off a tablespoonful of dough at a time and roll into a rope about 8 inches long. Coil the ends of rope inward to meet at the center, or twist them in opposite directions to form a coiled S shape. Then attach two shapes side by side. Or make smaller coils, using ½ tablespoon of dough, and put a few together. The important thing here is to be fanciful with your designs—and don't worry about being precise, as long as all your cookies are more or less the same size so they bake evenly. Press a whole almond into the center of each cookie and place them 3 inches apart on the greased baking sheets.

Bake the cookies for 10 to 15 minutes, or until browned at the edges. They should remain springy in the center, as they will firm somewhat as they cool. Cool on a rack.

MAKES ABOUT 2 DOZEN LARGE COOKIES

Made with the buttery hazelnuts that grow in Castiglione, near Messina, these crunchy (*croccante*) cookies contain just enough meringue to hold the nuts together. This is Chef Orazio's recipe from the Bar Saint Honoré in Taormina.

3½ cups hazelnuts

4 egg whites

2 cups sugar

¼ cup honey

1 teaspoon vanilla

¼ teaspoon cinnamon

Pinch of salt

Crispy Hazelnut Meringues
Croccantini

Preheat the oven to 350 degrees. Grease two baking sheets.

Spread the hazelnuts on a baking sheet and toast in the oven for about 20 minutes, or until fragrant and dark brown. (Err on the side of dark, for flavor's sake.) Allow them to cool, then rub them between the palms of your hands or a towel until most of the skins are removed. Roughly chop the hazelnuts and set aside.

In a heavy-bottomed saucepan over medium-low heat, whisk together the egg whites, sugar, honey, vanilla, cinnamon, and salt and cook, whisking constantly, until the mixture is thickened and opaque and most of the sugar is dissolved. Remove from the heat, stir in the hazelnuts, and allow to cool completely. (The batter can be kept, covered and refrigerated, for 1 day.)

Drop rounded tablespoonfuls of the batter 2 inches apart onto the greased baking sheet and bake for 25 to 30 minutes, or until deep golden brown. Allow the cookies to cool for 10 minutes before removing them from the pan, then cool on a rack. They will become crispy as they cool. Store in an airtight container.

MAKES ABOUT 3 DOZEN

Cookies and Small Pastries

Clove-Scented Chocolate Cookies

Tetù

One of the few Sicilian recipes that feature chocolate as their principal ingredient, these *tetù* call for cloves, an inspired addition. The combination is exotic, and it works. *Tetù* are traditional for All Souls' Day, commonly called *I Morti*, Day of the Dead, but nowadays they're sold year-round, especially in the western part of the island.

1 cup blanched whole almonds

4 cups unbleached all-purpose flour

8 tablespoons (1 stick) unsalted butter, softened

2 ounces unsweetened chocolate

1 cup milk

1½ cups sugar

1 teaspoon ground cloves

2 teaspoons baking soda

½ teaspoon salt

1 teaspoon vanilla

1 egg, beaten lightly to blend

GLAZE

2 cups sugar

1½ cups water

12 ounces unsweetened chocolate, roughly chopped

2 cups powdered sugar, sifted

Preheat the oven to 375 degrees.

Spread the almonds on a baking sheet and toast in the oven for 15 minutes to 20 minutes, or until well browned. Let cool. Grind the almonds to a coarse powder in a food processor or in a coffee grinder in small batches. Transfer to a large bowl, stir in the flour, and set aside.

In a medium saucepan over low heat, melt the butter, chocolate, and milk, whisking until the butter is melted. Whisk in the sugar, remove from the heat, and let cool to lukewarm.

Whisk the cloves, soda, salt, vanilla, and egg into the butter mixture. With a wooden spoon, stir the liquid ingredients into the flour-almond mixture just until combined. Chill the dough, covered, for 1 hour, or until easy to handle.

Preheat the oven to 375 degrees. Grease two baking sheets.

Pinch off a tablespoonful of the dough at a time, roll between the palms of your hands into smooth balls, and arrange 2 inches apart on the greased baking sheets.

Bake the cookies for 15 minutes, or until puffy but still slightly soft in the center. Allow the cookies to cool for 10 minutes before removing them from the pan.

Meanwhile, make the glaze: In a medium saucepan, bring the sugar and water to a boil, whisking constantly. Boil for 3 minutes, then remove from the heat and whisk in the chocolate until melted. Whisk in the powdered sugar until smooth.

While the cookies are still warm, immerse them, a few at a time, in the warm glaze, then place them on a cooling rack over a baking sheet to catch the drips. It's important that both the cookies and the glaze be warm so that some of the glaze soaks into the cookies. Cool on a rack.

MAKES ABOUT 3 DOZEN

Sweet Pastry Rings
Taralli all'Uovo

I'd always wondered how these got their unusually airy texture. The secret was revealed to me by a vendor at the street fair for *I Morti* in Palermo, where mountains of these cookies were being sold and consumed. They're boiled, then baked! These are often sold as *taralli all'uovo* to distinguish them from the savory yeast-risen variety of *taralli*.

> ¼ cup sugar
>
> 6 eggs
>
> ¼ cup vegetable oil
>
> 7 cups unbleached all-purpose flour
>
> ½ teaspoon salt
>
> 1 recipe Lemon Icing (glassa di limone; page 57)

In a large mixing bowl, with a wooden spoon, beat together the sugar, eggs, and oil until combined. Gradually stir in the flour and salt, mixing until the dough comes together. Knead gently on a floured surface for about 5 minutes, until smooth and satiny. Cover the dough and let it rest for 30 minutes.

Preheat the oven to 400 degrees. Grease three baking sheets or line them with parchment paper.

Pull off a piece of dough the size of a golf ball and roll it between the palms of your hands to form a rope about 6 inches long. Make another rope, then lay the ropes side by side on a floured board, twist them together, and join the ends to form a ring. Repeat with the remaining dough.

Meanwhile, bring 2 quarts of lightly salted water to a gentle boil in a large saucepan. When all the *taralli* are formed, drop them, a few at a time, into the water. When they begin to puff and rise to the surface, about 1 minute, turn them over and boil for an additional 3 minutes. Transfer the *taralli* with a slotted spoon to the prepared baking sheets.

Bake the *taralli* for 10 to 15 minutes, then turn the oven temperature down to 350 degrees and continue to bake for another 15 to 20 minutes, or until golden brown and firm to the touch. Remove from the oven and immediately brush them with the icing. Cool on a rack.

MAKES ABOUT 2 DOZEN

T here are many versions of this humble cookie, which dates back to Roman times. Some are made with cooked grape must syrup (*vino cotto*), others with honey. They are said to have been the "Power Bar" of the Roman army, given their nutritive value and long shelf life. This recipe comes from an eighteenth-century training manual for Benedictine monks. During the weeks preceding Christmas, when the requests for absolution were many, the overworked priests bucked up on these cookies, nutritious yet soft enough to eat silently, without betraying their presence, in the confessional.

Confessor's Cookies
Mostaccioli del Confessore

*2 cups whole wheat pastry flour, plus more if needed
   (found in health food stores and better supermarkets)*

*1 tablespoon finely chopped Candied Orange Peel
   (scorzetta d'arancia candita; page 193)*

⅓ cup honey

1 egg

2 tablespoons water

In a medium mixing bowl, combine the flour and orange peel. In a small bowl, stir together the honey, egg, and water. Add the flour mixture and stir until a firm dough forms. You may have to add a little more water or a bit more flour, a tablespoon at a time.

Turn the dough out onto a lightly floured work surface and knead vigorously until smooth. Let the dough rest, covered, for 1 hour.

Preheat the oven to 375 degrees. Grease a large baking sheet.

Pinch off a tablespoon of dough at a time and roll on a board into a 6-inch-long rope. With a very sharp knife, cut each rope into three 2-inch lengths.

Place the cookies 1 inch apart on the greased baking sheet and bake for 15 to 20 minutes, or until browned. Cool on a rack and store airtight.

MAKES ABOUT 3 DOZEN

*Cookies
and Small
Pastries*

Bones of the Dead
Ossa dei Morti

For reasons I don't understand, these rock-hard cookies are dearly beloved by Sicilians of all ages (and it doesn't even seem to require a mouth full of teeth to enjoy them). Most commonly called "bones of the dead" for their matte-white appearance, they show up in pastry shops around the end of October, just in time for *I Morti,* All Souls' Day. They change hats around Eastertime, becoming *agnelli pasquali semplici,* or simple Easter lambs, referring to an earlier time in Sicilian history, when the poor of the eastern part of the island made these in place of the elaborate marzipan lambs of the west. History notwithstanding, they seem to hold the same promise of conquest that jaw-breakers do in the United States, perhaps explaining their popular appeal. Bones of the Dead are pictured in the background of the photograph on page 68.

> *2½ cups unbleached all-purpose flour*
>
> *2 cups sugar*
>
> *¾ teaspoon ground cloves*
>
> *⅓ cup water*

Sift together the flour, sugar, and cloves into a large heavy saucepan. Whisk in the water until a rather stiff paste forms, set the pan over medium heat, and, stirring constantly with a wooden spoon, cook the paste for 5 minutes, until very hot. Do not scrape up any dry bits that cling to the bottom of the pan; the paste should be very smooth. Turn the paste out onto a work surface lightly dusted with flour. Shape it into a rough square about ½ inch thick, and allow to cool completely.

When the paste is cool, cut it into 24 diamond shapes with a very sharp knife. Transfer to a wooden board, or other porous surface, that has been lightly dusted with flour to prevent sticking, leaving 1 inch between the cookies. Now you must be patient, because the unbaked cookies need to dry out for 3 days, uncovered. In a dry place, of course.

At the end of the third day, preheat the oven to 325 degrees. Lightly grease three baking sheets. Have ready a small bowl of hot water.

Remove the cookies one at a time from the board, dip the bottoms in the hot water for the count of 10, and place 3 inches apart on the prepared baking sheets.

Bake for about 25 minutes, or until the sugar melts and forms a caramel-colored puddle at the base of each cookie but the tops remain white and firm. (The puddle is part of the cookie.) Allow to cool completely before removing from the pans. The cookies will harden as they cool.

MAKES 2 DOZEN

Antica Dolceria Bonajuto

MODICA

Modican chocolate is unparalleled in savor, such that tasting it is like reaching
the archetype, the absolute, and that chocolate produced elsewhere, even the
most celebrated, is an adulteration, a corruption of the original.

La Contea di Modica, LEONARDO SCIASCIA

Customers speak in reverential whispers at the Antica Dolceria Bonajuto. Here in the stately Baroque town of Modica, Signor Franco Ruta and his family have upheld the tradition of *original* Modican chocolate since 1880. You can feel the weight of history as you enter the shop, even before the aromas of chocolate, cinnamon, and vanilla come wafting toward you.

In the early sixteenth century, the town of Modica was home base for a large population of wealthy Spanish nobles who, at the time, were also colonizing Mexico. In the New World, they encountered myriad new foods, among which was *xocolatl,* made from ground cacao beans using a laborious process developed by the Aztecs. *Xocolatl* was eaten in solid form and as a beverage and enjoyed as a stimulant and for the feeling of euphoria it was thought to induce. The Spaniards liked it too. They named it *cioccolato,* the masculine form of the word

(deeming it masculine for its cigar shape), and brought it home to Sicily, along with the secret Aztec recipe. This recipe never traveled far beyond Modica, the only city in the province wealthy enough to afford both the costly importation of cacao beans from Mexico and the traditional method of production.

Continuing to use the Aztec method, with cacao imported from the Ivory Coast and the help of a few modern tools, the Bonajuto chocolate remains true to its roots. During the heating process the mixture is kept below 120 degrees, just hot enough for the cocoa butter, but not the sugar, to melt. The resulting product has the lushness of chocolate with a pleasant crunch to the teeth.

The Dolceria is as much a museum as a shop. Signor Ruta and his son Pierpaolo have created meticulous still lifes in the glass-front mahogany cabinets that line the walls of the reception room, all bearing witness to a centuries-old culinary tradition, curated tenderly by the Rutas.

Chocolate takes on many personalities here. It is made into a thick, spicy beverage similar in flavor and texture to Mexican hot chocolate. Tiny trufflelike sweets are bathed in the stuff, and a lighter-than-air *gelo di cioccolato* is flavored with chocolate and thickened with wheat starch. Remaining true to the old recipes, the Rutas use no butter or dairy in any of their sweets.

By far the most intriguing way in which chocolate is put to use here is in the pastries known as *impanatigghe* and their cousins, the *lucumie*. *Impanatigghe* are sweet pastries filled with ground beef, almonds, sugar, honey, cinnamon, and chocolate. *Lucumie* are the poor man's version, with eggplant taking the place of beef.

Both have their roots in sixteenth-century Spain. The name *impanatigghe* (pronounced "im-pan-a-tee-gay") is a corruption of the Spanish word *empanadilla,* referring to a small pastry containing a filling. The *empanadilla* in question had a filling that is still popular in Latin America today, made with meat, almonds, cinnamon, raisins, and olives. The Sicilian Spaniards sweetened the mixture, adding chocolate and honey and subtracting the olives and onions, until the savory *empanadilla* became the sweet *impanatigghe.*

It is exciting to see how, with intelligent use of modern technology, the Rutas have taken up the task of bringing these traditions to the attention of a global audience. Pierpaolo has created an informative and bilingual Web site. (www.ragusaonline.com/ bonajuto) and is currently researching a documentary on the history of chocolate in general and Modican chocolate in particular.

At last, the world beyond this tiny province will know the archetypal chocolate that the people of Modica have enjoyed for more than five hundred years.

Meat and Chocolate Pastries
Impanatigghe

DOUGH

    4½ cups unbleached all-purpose flour

    6 tablespoons sugar

    ½ tablespoon salt

    ½ pound (2 sticks) unsalted butter or margarine, chilled

    1 egg

    6 tablespoons sweet wine, such as Marsala

FILLING

    ½ pound lean ground sirloin

    One 8-ounce jar unsalted roasted almond butter
        (available at health food stores and some large supermarkets)

    3 ounces unsweetened chocolate, chopped

    ½ cup sugar

    ½ teaspoon cinnamon

    2 teaspoons vanilla

    ½ cup thyme honey (see Sources)

    3 egg whites

For the Dough

Sift together the flour, sugar, and salt into a large mixing bowl. Cut in the chilled butter or margarine until the mixture resembles coarse cornmeal. In a small bowl, beat together the egg and wine just to blend, then add all at once to the flour mixture, tossing together until the dough forms a ball.

Transfer the dough to a lightly floured work surface and knead gently a few times until smooth. Wrap the dough in plastic and chill while you make the filling.

For the Filling

In a medium skillet, sauté the beef over medium heat, stirring to break up any large lumps, until it is no longer pink. Drain and transfer to a food processor fitted with the steel blade. Immediately add the remaining ingredients and process until the mixture forms a very smooth paste.

For the Pastries

Preheat the oven to 350 degrees. Divide the dough into quarters. Work with one piece of dough at a time, keeping the remainder covered. On a lightly floured work surface, roll out each piece very thin (no thicker than ⅛ inch). With a 3-inch cookie cutter, cut out circles of dough. Place a teaspoonful of the filling in the center of each, moisten the edges with a little water, and fold over. Pinch the edges together to seal and trim the edges with a fluted pastry wheel. Reroll the scraps of dough to make more circles.

Place the pastries 2 inches apart on ungreased baking sheets and bake for 15 to 20 minutes, or until light golden brown. Cool on a rack.

MAKES ABOUT 4 DOZEN

Eggplant and Chocolate Pastries

Lucumie

DOUGH

    4½ cups unbleached all-purpose flour

    6 tablespoons sugar

    ½ teaspoon salt

    ½ pound (2 sticks) unsalted butter or margarine, chilled

    1 egg

    6 tablespoons sweet wine, such as Marsala

FILLING

    1 large eggplant (about ¾ pound)

    2 tablespoons vegetable oil

    One 8-ounce jar unsalted roasted almond butter
        (available in health food stores and some large supermarkets)

    2 ounces unsweetened chocolate, chopped

    ¼ cup sugar

    ½ teaspoon cinnamon

    2 teaspoons vanilla

    ½ cup thyme honey (see Sources)

Preheat the oven to 400 degrees.

For the Dough

Sift together the flour, sugar, and salt into a large mixing bowl. Cut in the chilled butter or margarine until the mixture resembles coarse cornmeal. In a small bowl, beat together the egg and wine just to blend, then add all at once to the flour mixture, tossing together until the dough forms a ball.

Transfer the dough to a lightly floured work surface and knead gently a few times until smooth. Wrap the dough in plastic wrap and chill while you make the filling.

For the Filling

Cut the eggplant in half. Brush the cut side with the vegetable oil and place cut side down on a baking sheet. Bake until very soft, about 25 to 30 minutes. Let cool until easy to handle.

Scrape out 2 cups of the eggplant flesh, and discard the seeds and skin. Place the eggplant flesh and the remaining ingredients in a food processor fitted with the steel blade and process continuously until the mixture forms a very smooth paste.

For the Pastries

Reduce the oven temperature to 350 degrees. Divide the dough into quarters. Work with one piece of dough at a time, keeping the remainder covered. On a lightly floured work surface, roll out each piece very thin (no thicker than ⅛ inch). With a 3-inch cookie cutter, cut out circles of dough. Place a teaspoonful of filling in the center of each, moisten the edges with a little water, and fold over. Pinch the edges together to seal and trim the edges with a fluted pastry wheel. Reroll the scraps of dough to make more circles.

Place the pastries 2 inches apart on ungreased baking sheets and bake for 15 to 20 minutes, or until light golden brown. Cool on a rack.

MAKES ABOUT 4 DOZEN

Virgin's Breasts
Minni della Vergine

Sicilians are serious about body parts. Take Saint Agatha, the patron saint of Catania, who sliced off her breasts in martyrdom and is depicted forever- more carrying them on a plate. The pastries called virgin's breasts were created in her honor by the sisters of the Monastero della Vergine in Palermo and later adopted by the Catanians, who, in the interest of anatomical correctness, added the cherry on top. Virgin's breasts are eaten with reverence at the Feast of Saint Agatha, which takes place in Catania every year on February third to the fifth. Elsewhere in Sicily, you will frequently see miniature *cassatas,* or *cassatine,* sporting a cherry garnish. In this case, they too may be called virgin's breasts.

1 recipe Milk Pudding (biancomangiare; page 174), cooled

¼ cup Squash Preserves (zuccata; page 190) or Candied Orange Peel (scorzetta d'arancia candita; page 193), roughly chopped, optional

1 teaspoon cinnamon

2 ounces semisweet chocolate, roughly chopped

1 recipe Sweet Pastry Dough (pasta frolla; page 62)

1 recipe Sugar Icing (glassa di zucchero; page 55)

16 candied cherries

Preheat the oven to 375 degrees.

Mix the milk pudding with the squash preserves or candied orange peel (if using), cinnamon, and chocolate. Set aside.

On a lightly floured work surface, roll out the pastry dough ⅛ inch thick. Cut out 16 circles using a 2-inch cookie cutter and 16 more circles using a 3- or 4-inch cutter. Place a good mound of the filling on top of each of the smaller circles of dough, so that it resembles a breast. Moisten the edges of dough with a little water or egg white, place one of the larger pieces of dough on top to fully enclose the filling, and press the edges to seal.

Place the pastries 2 inches apart on ungreased baking sheets and bake for 15 to 20 minutes, or until golden brown. Cool on a rack.

When the pastries are cool, pour sugar icing over each one and immediately place a cherry you-know-where.

Makes 16

Engagement Cookies

Nacatuli

These elegant little cookies carry profound symbolism for the people of Lipari. Served at engagement parties accompanied by the island's famous Malvasia wine, they are believed to sweeten the occasion and ensure a good result for the marriage. This recipe is from Bar Oscar, where the two Adele sisters show up twice a week to turn out hundreds of *nacatuli* in traditional shapes: roses for love, fish for good luck, and suggestively shaped ovals for fertility.

DOUGH

2 cups unbleached all-purpose flour

¼ cup sugar

4 tablespoons (½ stick) unsalted butter, chilled

¼ cup Malvasia or other sweet wine

2 egg yolks

FILLING

1 cup blanched whole almonds, toasted and finely ground

¼ cup plus 2 tablespoons sugar

½ teaspoon cinnamon

2 tablespoons Tangerine Liqueur (mandarinetto; page 199), orange liqueur, or orange juice

For the Dough

Sift together the flour and sugar into a medium bowl. Cut in the butter until the mixture resembles coarse cornmeal. In a small bowl, beat together the wine and egg yolks until blended. Pour the wine and egg mixture into the flour mixture and toss together until the dough forms a ball.

Turn the dough out onto a lightly floured work surface and knead gently for about 5 minutes, or until smooth. Wrap in plastic wrap and refrigerate while you make the filling.

For the Filling

In a medium bowl, mix all the ingredients together to form a paste. Cover and set aside.

For the Cookies

Preheat the oven to 375 degrees.

This is like making ravioli: Divide the dough into quarters. Work with one piece at a time, keeping the remainder covered. On a lightly floured work surface, roll out one piece of dough as thin as you can, approximately 12 inches long and 2 inches wide. Drop about 12 mounds of filling (about 1 teaspoonful each) down the length of the dough, 1 inch apart and ¼ inch from the edge of the dough. Roll out another piece of dough to the same dimensions and place on top of the first sheet. Using a fluted pastry wheel, cut between the mounds of filled dough to make individual pastries in various shapes. Press around the mounds of filling to seal the dough. Place them 2 inches apart on an ungreased baking sheet. With a sharp small pair of scissors, cut several small incisions in the top of each to expose the filling. Be as creative as you like. If you are feeling particularly ambitious, you can coil little strips of dough cut from the scraps to make roses, and press them into the tops of the pastries, attaching them with a bit of water or beaten egg white. Repeat with the remaining dough and filling.

Bake the *nacatuli* for 10 to 15 minutes, or until lightly golden. Cool on a rack.

MAKES ABOUT 2 DOZEN

Citrus-Filled Almond Pillows
Cuscinetti

Here is one of the more ubiquitous pastries of the island—and another great use for the almond paste you've so devotedly made.

1 egg yolk

1 recipe Almond Paste (pasta di mandorle; page 59)

¾ cup Citron Preserves (conserva di cedro; page 193) or best-quality citrus marmalade

½ cup powdered sugar, divided

Preheat the oven to 350 degrees. Grease two large baking sheets.

In a large mixing bowl, using your hands or a wooden spoon, work the yolk into the almond paste until well combined.

Turn the dough out onto a work surface that has been lightly dusted with some of the powdered sugar, and divide into 4 equal pieces. Pat each piece into a rectangle about 8 inches long by 3 inches wide. Spread one-quarter of the preserves lengthwise down the center of the dough and fold the sides over to enclose the filling, overlapping slightly. (If the dough cracks, just dip your fingers in a little water and pinch it back together.) With a sharp knife, cut each log into 8 equal pieces.

Place the pieces 2 inches apart on the greased baking sheets. Sift the remaining powdered sugar over the cookies and bake for 20 to 25 minutes, or until golden brown.

MAKES 32

Santa Lucia, the patron saint of eyes, is the protectress of Siracusa. She is credited with having twice during Roman times saved the city from famine. The first time, she performed this miracle in the winter by sending shiploads of grain, and the second time, in the spring, by sending flocks of quails or doves. Two miracles merit two feasts, so she is honored in December and again in May.

These cookies were created twenty-five years ago for the May feast of Santa Lucia by the late Ernesto Marciante, whose sons Giuseppe and Valerio carry on in his spirit at the Pasticceria Marciante in Siracusa.

> *1 recipe Almond Paste (pasta di mandorle; page 59)*
>
> *½ cup golden raisins, roughly chopped*
>
> *2 teaspoons grated orange zest*
>
> *½ teaspoon baking powder*
>
> *Twelve 2 by 1-inch strips Candied Orange Peel*
> *   (scorzetta d'arancia candita; page 193), or fresh zest*
>
> *About ½ cup sifted powdered sugar*

Preheat the oven to 375 degrees. Grease two baking sheets.

In a large mixing bowl, with clean hands, knead the almond paste until pliable. Knead in the raisins, orange zest, and baking powder.

Divide the dough into 24 pieces and shape each piece into a flat oval about ½ inch thick with pointed ends, to resemble an eye. With a ½-inch-round cookie cutter, cut 2 circles out of each strip of orange peel and press them into the center of the "eyes." Be gentle—these are the eyeballs.

Place the cookies 2 inches apart on the greased baking sheets and dust generously with powdered sugar. Bake for 15 to 20 minutes, or until golden brown. Cool on a rack.

Makes 2 dozen

Cookies and Small Pastries

Chewy Almond Cookies
Fior di Mandorla

I t's a rare *pasticceria* that doesn't feature these soft, chewy cookies, popular throughout Sicily. From Milazzo, take the short hydrofoil ride to the Aeolian island of Lipari and go straight to the Pasticceria Subba—their *fior di mandorla* are puffy and sweet and perfect with a glass of the island's famous Malvasia wine.

1 recipe Almond Paste (pasta di mandorle; page 59)
¾ teaspoon baking powder
¾ cup powdered sugar, divided

Grease two baking sheets. In a large mixing bowl or a food processor fitted with the steel blade, mix or process the almond paste with the baking powder until the dough comes together in a ball. Dust a work surface lightly with half of the powdered sugar and turn the dough out onto it. Knead gently for about 1 minute, or until smooth.

Break off tablespoonfuls of dough, form them into rough S shapes, and place them 2 inches apart on the greased baking sheets. Sift the remaining powdered sugar over the cookies and allow them to sit at room temperature for 1 hour before baking.

Preheat the oven to 375 degrees.

Bake the cookies for 20 to 25 minutes, or until golden brown. Let cool for 10 minutes before removing them from the pans.

MAKES ABOUT 30

Giuseppe Chemi of Pasticceria Etna in Taormina makes these cookies with the luscious bright green pistachios grown in nearby Bronte, on the slopes of Mount Etna.

2 cups shelled raw pistachios

1⅓ cups blanched whole almonds

2 cups sugar

¾ teaspoon baking powder

Pinch of salt

2 eggs, beaten lightly to blend

2 tablespoons honey

2 teaspoons vanilla

1 teaspoon grated orange zest

½ cup powdered sugar, divided

Chewy Pistachio Cookies
Fior di Pistacchio

Preheat the oven to 250 degrees.

In a large saucepan, bring 2 quarts of water to boil. Plunge the pistachios into the boiling water and immediately remove the pan from the heat. Let the pistachios sit in the water for 3 minutes, then drain them and rinse well with cold water. Rub them in a towel, in several batches, drying them and removing the purplish skin at the same time. Don't worry if all the skins don't come off, but a little effort is worth a lot in this case.

Spread the pistachios in a single layer on a baking sheet and dry them in the oven for 20 to 25 minutes. Allow them to cool completely before grinding.

In a food processor fitted with the steel blade, in 2 batches grind the pistachios, almonds, and sugar to a fine powder. Return all the mixture to the processor along with the baking powder and salt. Pulse to combine. Then with the machine running, add the remaining ingredients except the powdered sugar and process until the dough comes together in a ball.

Grease two baking sheets. Turn the dough onto a work surface lightly dusted with some of the powdered sugar. Knead gently for about 1 minute, or until smooth. Break off tablespoonfuls of the dough and roll them between the palms of your hands into chubby 2-inch-long logs. Place them 2 inches apart on the greased baking sheets and flatten them slightly. Sift the remaining powdered sugar over the cookies and allow them to sit at room temperature for 1 hour before baking.

Preheat the oven to 375 degrees.

Bake the cookies for 20 to 25 minutes, or until light golden brown. Cool for 10 minutes before removing them from the baking sheets.

MAKES ABOUT 30

Conchiglie belong to the category of sweets known as *dolci di badia,* or abbey sweets. Leaving the Badia Santo Spirito in Agrigento with a package of cookies the nuns had so devotedly prepared, we met a young boy carrying his macho tabby cat down the hill. I unwrapped the cookies and offered him one. After careful consideration, the boy chose the most beautiful one, a *conchiglia,* thanked us, and fed it to his cat!

Filled Marzipan Seashells
Conchiglie

Cornstarch for the molds

½ recipe Marzipan (pasta reale; page 61)

Yellow, red, and green food coloring, optional

¼ cup Citron Preserves (conserva di cedro; page 189, Pistachio Preserves (conserva di pistacchi; page 188), or best-quality citrus marmalade

You will need 12 plastic candy molds in a 2-inch seashell shape to make these (see Sources). Dust them lightly with cornstarch.

If you would like a marbled effect, divide the marzipan into 2 or 3 pieces and tint each piece with a different food color. Then, on a work surface lightly dusted with cornstarch, gently knead the pieces together until the colors are swirled.

Divide the marzipan into 24 equal pieces and cover them with a piece of plastic wrap or a damp towel to prevent their drying out. Press 1 piece of marzipan into each of the molds, covering the bottoms of the forms. Drop a teaspoon of the preserves into each lined mold and dab the edges of the marzipan lightly with water to moisten.

Dust your hands with cornstarch and pat out the remaining pieces of marzipan so they are big enough to cover the tops of the molds. Attach these to the moistened bottoms and press to secure. Turn the molds upside down and release the shells.

With a dry pastry brush, brush off any cornstarch clinging to them. Allow them to dry for 1 hour. These can be stored airtight for up to 3 days.

Makes 1 dozen

T
hroughout Sicily, gifts of candy and confections are given to, and exchanged by, engaged couples to sweeten the outcome of their marriage. The *innamorati* of Noto exchange these little pink hearts, lovingly created by Corrado Costanzo in his shop on the Via Spaventa.

Marzipan Engagement Hearts
Cuoricini per i Fidanzati

1 teaspoon rose water

Red food coloring

½ recipe Marzipan (pasta reale; page 61)

Cornstarch for the pan

*Royal Icing (glassa reale; below) or
    prepared white frosting*

Work the rose water and enough red food coloring into the marzipan so it is as rosy as you wish. Cover the marzipan to keep it from drying out. One at a time, pinch off tablespoonfuls of dough and shape them into little hearts, flattening them to ½ inch thick. Place the hearts on a sheet of parchment or waxed paper that has been dusted with a little cornstarch to keep it from sticking. (Or roll out the marzipan on a cornstarch-dusted work surface to ½ inch thick and cut out shapes with a small heart-shaped cookie cutter. Gather up and reroll the scraps.)

When all the hearts have been formed, fit a pastry bag with a writing tip, fill with the icing, and write whatever sweet nothings your heart desires on the *cuoricini*.

MAKES ABOUT 2 DOZEN

Royal Icing Glassa Reale

1 egg white

2 to 3 cups powdered sugar

In a small bowl, whip the egg white until foamy. Whisk in the sugar a little at a time until the icing is stiff enough to hold its shape. Keep covered with plastic wrap until ready to use. The icing lasts 3 days if stored airtight.

MAKES ABOUT 1 CUP

*Cookies
and Small
Pastries*

Marzipan Fruit
FRUTTA DI MARTORANA

Sicilians love a good joke.

So it happened that a certain Mother Superior from the Convent of the Martorana in Palermo staged an elaborate prank for the Archbishop's Easter visit. The nuns in the convent kitchen were instructed to fashion dozens of fruits made of *pasta reale,* marzipan, painting them to mimic the real thing. Just before the Archbishop's arrival, the fruits were hung from the trees in the cloister garden. So lifelike were they that the Archbishop was fooled into thinking a miracle had caused all the trees to bear fruit in one season!

The Convent of the Martorana, named in honor of its elegant patroness, Eloisa Martorana, used to be a part of the Church of Santa Maria dell'Ammiraglio in Palermo. The convent is long gone, but the church, built in the mosaic-rich Arab-Norman style, lives on.

So deeply engrained is this story in the Sicilian memory that realistic fruits, vegetables, and all manner of *trompe l'oeil* masterpieces made of marzipan are commonly called *martorana.* Although *martorana* are now a permanent fixture throughout the year, autumn is the time when pastry artists pull out all the stops.

November 2 is *I Morti,* All Souls' Day. Sicilian children awake to find baskets of *martorana* left for them by their ancestors who have passed on. Later, entire families gather at the cemeteries to feast on these and other foods in communion with their dearly departed. So, by the end of each October, all the pastry shops are filled with startlingly realistic fruits and vegetables. The really ambitious and creative among them turn out masterpieces of seafood, street food, *cannoli,* balls of provolone on a string, even spaghetti and marinara sauce, all fashioned entirely of marzipan.

At this time of year, there is a carnival in the streets of Palermo to celebrate *I Morti.* It's as loud and flashy as anything you'll see, with stall after stall overflowing with displays of *martorana* in every conceivable design. Mountains of cookies and slabs of neon-colored nougat, called *gelato di campagna,* share tent space with plastic toys, hair ornaments, and socks. Mariano Scurato has the flashiest of all *martorana* booths, and he claims to sell more than two hundred pounds of *martorana* the evening of November 1.

The fair is also where you will find the hand-painted sugar statues called *pupi di cena,* which will show up in the *I Morti* baskets along with the *martorana.* Knights on horseback, kings, queens, devils, and peasant girls stand proudly alongside Smurfs, Donald Duck, and Spider-Man. The *pupi* in Sicily are presented in the same spirit as the sugar skulls of Mexico's *Dia de las Muertas.* It seems likely that this is a cross-pollination of the Spaniards.

The crafting of *martorana* is a three-day process. Over the years, I have followed several of Sicily's most talented pastry artists through the stages of production. There was universal agreement as to the method, and laborious though it is, with a little dexterity and creativity, anyone can do it.

+ *Day 1:* Blanch and peel the almonds if necessary, then grind them to make the marzipan (*pasta reale;* page 61). Shape the marzipan into whatever forms you wish and place them on racks to dry.

+ *Day 2:* Using liquid food coloring diluted with vodka or water, paint the *martorana.* Return them to the racks to dry again.

+ *Day 3:* Dilute powdered gum arabic (see Sources) with water, and glaze the *martorana.* Put them back on the racks until the glaze is dry. *Martorana* made in this manner can be stored airtight for as long as 3 months.

D emand for *martorana* is so great that some artists have resorted to shaping theirs with the aid of plaster molds, although the dexterous work just as quickly by hand. Maria Grammatico, renowned for the beauty of her *martorana*, often uses two thousand pounds of almonds a month, which works out to 150 pieces a day—and that's during low season!

With decorative plasterwork as refined as it is in Sicily, it is not difficult to find a *gessaio*, or plaster worker, in the larger cities. Most of them carry ready-made *martorana* molds, or will make some for you with a few days' notice. In the United States, there is a product called "casting gel" that you can use to make molds of your own (see Sources), or you can try your hand with plaster of Paris. If you make plaster molds, they must be sealed with a coat of latex varnish before using. In any case, dust the molds lightly with cornstarch to prevent the marzipan paste from sticking.

Fancy Little Pastries
Dolcini di Erice

These little beauties belong to the family of sweets known as *dolci di riposto,* or cupboard sweets— showy little confections that can be bought in bulk and kept in the cupboard for unexpected guests. *Dolci di riposto* are also served at weddings and important social occasions. This recipe (pictured on page 64) is from the Pasticceria Colicchia in Trapani.

½ recipe Sweet Pastry Dough (pasta frolla; page 62)

1½ cups Citron Preserves (conserva di cedro; page 189)

1 recipe Marzipan (pasta reale; page 61)

Cornstarch for dusting

Assorted food colorings

1 recipe Sugar Icing (glassa di zucchero; page 55)

Preheat the oven to 400 degrees.

On a lightly floured work surface, roll out the pastry dough to a thickness of ¼ inch. Cut it into various shapes with 2-inch cookie cutters. Place the shapes 2 inches apart on ungreased baking sheets.

Bake for 12 to 15 minutes, or until golden brown. Let cool. These will form the bases of the pastries.

Place a spoonful of preserves on top of each cooled base. On a work surface dusted lightly with cornstarch, roll out the marzipan to a thickness of ¼ inch. With the same cookie cutters, cut shapes to match the bases. Separate the pieces and roll out each one to ⅛ inch thick, keeping its shape. Press these on top of the filled cookie bases to cover the filling; you may have to dab a little water on the edges of the marzipan to seal it to the base. If you are feeling particularly creative, cut out additional decorations from the marzipan scraps with tiny cookie or aspic cutters and attach them to the tops.

Allow the *dolcini* to dry for 1 day, loosely covered, then paint the pastries with a small amount of food coloring diluted in cold water. The design is up to you.

Allow them to dry for 1 more day, then glaze the tops by brushing them with the icing.

MAKES ABOUT 2 DOZEN

T he Feast of Saint Agatha, patroness of Catania, is celebrated during the first week of February. Like the pastries made to resemble her breasts cut off in martyrdom, these marzipan olives represent a legend. Agatha, knowing she was unable to escape death, grasped the branch of a sterile olive tree. From the contact with her hand, the tree became fertile, blossomed, and bore fruit.

Saint Agatha's Little Olives
Olivette di Sant'Agata

Green food coloring
½ recipe Marzipan (pasta reale; page 61)
⅓ cup superfine sugar

Work enough food coloring into the marzipan to make it a deep but bright green color. Divide the marzipan into 24 equal pieces and cover them with plastic wrap or a damp towel to prevent their drying out.

One at a time, roll each piece into an olive shape between the palms of your hands, then roll in the superfine sugar and place on a baking sheet or tray. Allow to dry for 1 hour, then store airtight for up to 1 month.

MAKES 2 DOZEN

Cream Puffs
Bignè

The name *bignè* (sounds like "been-yay") comes from the French word *beignet*, or fritter. A Sicilian *bignè* is baked, and it closely resembles a cream puff. When fried, it is known as *sfinci*.

I recommend that you use margarine instead of butter in this dough. What you lose in flavor will be more than made up for by the gain in texture—margarine produces *bignè* that are all crispness and light, while butter produces a rather more heavy version. It's your choice.

> 8 tablespoons (1 stick) unsalted margarine, cut into ½-inch cubes
>
> ¾ cup water
>
> 1 tablespoon sugar
>
> Pinch of salt
>
> 1 cup unbleached all-purpose flour
>
> 4 eggs
>
> Ice cream, whipped cream, or 1 recipe Pastry Cream
> (crema pasticciera; page 50)
>
> Sugar Icing (glassa di zucchero; page 55), Chocolate Icing (glassa di cioccolato;
> page 56), or Lemon Icing (glassa di limone; page 57), optional

In a medium heavy-bottomed saucepan, bring the margarine, water, sugar, and salt to a boil, stirring with a wooden spoon until the margarine is melted. Remove from the heat and add the flour all at once, stirring with gusto until the dough forms a ball that pulls away from the sides of the pan. Allow to cool, stirring every now and then to release the steam, for 15 minutes.

Preheat the oven to 425 degrees. Lightly grease two large baking sheets.

Beat the eggs one at a time into the dough, making sure that each one is well incorporated before adding the next. The dough should be loose but not runny. Spoon out rounded tablespoonfuls of the dough and place 3 inches apart on the lightly greased baking sheets. Don't worry about making them look perfect at this point—as they bake, they will blossom dramatically and come into their own beauty.

Sprinkle a little bit of water over them (or use a spray bottle) and bake them for 15 minutes, *without opening the oven,* or they will collapse. Turn the oven temperature down to 350 degrees and bake for an additional 30 minutes or so. Now you can peek, but don't allow the oven door to slam shut. The *bignè* are done when they are firm and dry and sound hollow when you tap them lightly. Allow them to cool completely before filling with ice cream, whipped cream, or pastry cream. If desired, top with the icing of your choice. (*Bignè* can be made ahead of time and frozen in airtight containers. Crisp them on a baking sheet in a preheated 400-degree oven for 5 minutes and allow them to cool before filling.)

MAKES ABOUT 30

Sicilian Cream Puffs with Two Fillings

Lulus

More than just buxom *bigné*, the *lulus* at the Pasticceria Vinci Domenico in Messina are bursting with a lusty filling of whipped cream with vanilla or chocolate and hazelnuts. It's not hard to imagine why they were given such a coquettish name.

8 tablespoons (1 stick) unsalted margarine, cut into ½-inch cubes

¾ cup water

1 tablespoon sugar

Pinch of salt

1 cup unbleached all-purpose flour

4 eggs

Vanilla Filling (crema alla panna; below) or Chocolate-Hazelnut Filling (gianduia; below)

In a medium heavy-bottomed saucepan, bring the margarine, water, sugar, and salt to a boil, stirring with a wooden spoon until the margarine is melted. Remove from the heat and add the flour all at once, stirring with gusto until the dough forms a ball that pulls away from the sides of the pan. Allow the dough to cool, stirring every now and then to release the steam, for 15 minutes.

Preheat the oven to 425 degrees. Lightly grease six 2½-inch custard cups or muffin cups.

Beat the eggs one at a time into the dough, making sure that each one is well incorporated before adding the next. The dough should be loose but not runny. Spoon the dough evenly into the prepared custard cups. Don't worry about making the tops too smooth at this point; they will blossom dramatically as they bake and become beautiful on their own.

Sprinkle a little bit of water over them (or use a spray bottle) and bake for 15 minutes, *without opening the oven,* or they will collapse. Turn the oven temperature down to 350 degrees and bake for another 40 minutes or so. You can peek after 30 minutes, but don't allow the oven door to slam shut. The *lulus* are ready when they are firm and dry and sound hollow when you tap the tops lightly. Allow them to cool completely before filling with the vanilla or chocolate filling. (You can make these ahead of time and freeze them airtight. Crisp them on a baking sheet in a preheated 400-degree oven for 5 minutes and allow them to cool before filling.)

MAKES 6

Vanilla Filling Crema alla Panna

2 cups heavy whipping cream

¾ cup powdered sugar, divided

2 teaspoons vanilla

½ teaspoon grated lemon zest

In a large chilled bowl, whip the cream with ½ cup of the powdered sugar, the vanilla, and zest until stiff. (But don't go too far, or you will make butter.) Fit a 14-inch pastry bag with a large plain tip (or no tip at all) and fill with the whipped cream. Poke a hole in the bottom of each *lulu* and squeeze the filling in with the pastry bag. Dust the tops with the remaining ¼ cup powdered sugar and serve immediately, or refrigerate for up to 3 hours.

MAKES ABOUT 4 CUPS, OR ENOUGH TO FILL 6 LULUS

Chocolate Hazelnut Filling Gianduia

One 8-ounce jar Nutella (chocolate-hazelnut cream)

1½ cups heavy whipping cream, divided

1 teaspoon vanilla

*6 tablespoons powdered milk chocolate or semisweet chocolate—not cocoa
(Ghirardelli makes a good product; see Sources)*

In a small bowl, whisk together the Nutella and ½ cup of the cream.

In a large chilled bowl, whip the remaining 1 cup cream with the vanilla until soft peaks form. Stir in the Nutella mixture and continue to whip until stiff. Fill the *lulus* as for the vanilla filling, above, and dust the tops with the powdered chocolate. Serve immediately, or refrigerate for up to 3 hours.

MAKES ABOUT 4 CUPS, OR ENOUGH TO FILL 6 LULUS

Fried Pastries

Frittelle

$\mathcal{S}$icilians aren't afraid of a little fat. It makes things taste good.

Go to any *fiera*, or street fair, in Sicily and you'll find a crowd around the huge kettles of bubbling fat (usually lard), waiting for the *frittelle* to emerge, browned, tender, and crispy.

In the town of Floridia, just outside Siracusa, a festival in celebration of the new wine takes place at the beginning of November. A mammoth cask of the season's first wine is wheeled into the *piazza*, the priest blesses and uncorks it, and for about seventy-five cents, you (and the entire population of Floridia) can buy a plastic cup to catch the wine as it gushes out. This is the sign for the men to begin grilling huge coils of sausages and the women to fry the *zeppole*, delicious little sugar-dusted fritters the size of doughnut holes. They are addictive.

Opposite: Krapfen, *page 133*

If eating fried pastries scares you, I understand. Once, in a Sicilian *trattoria*, I asked if they had any low-calorie desserts. (What was I thinking?) *"Si, certo, signorina!"* I was given a pear and a knife.

The really brave among us should try frying the Sicilian way—in lard. It produces a pastry that is melt-in-your-mouth light and crispy, and not at all greasy. Besides, as they say in Sicily: *"Quannu 'na cosa piaci nun fa dannu"* (That which gives pleasure does not do harm).

A t Bar di Noto in Piana degli Albanesi, size is a relative concept. The *maxi cannoli* are as big as an arm, and these *ravioli* are the size of a plate. They are the perfect vehicles for the tangy local ricotta, which lurks inside both of them. The use of lard (or shortening) in this recipe makes a pastry that is melt-in-your-mouth light and crispy.

Sweet Ricotta Turnovers
Ravioli di Ricotta

> 4½ cups unbleached all-purpose flour
>
> ¼ cup sugar
>
> ¼ teaspoon salt
>
> ½ cup lard or vegetable shortening, chilled and cut into ½-inch cubes
>
> ½ to ¾ cup sweet wine, such as Marsala
>
> 2½ cups Ricotta Cream (crema di ricotta; page 54)
>
> Lard or vegetable oil for frying
>
> Powdered sugar for dusting

In a large bowl, stir together the flour, sugar, and salt. With your fingertips, rub in the lard or shortening until the mixture resembles coarse cornmeal. Add the wine a tablespoon at a time until the dough begins to come together.

Transfer the dough to a lightly floured work surface and knead until smooth and satiny. Cover with a damp towel and let rest in a cool place for an hour. Divide the dough into 2 pieces.

On a floured surface, roll out each piece of dough very thin, to about ¹⁄₁₆ inch. Cut into 10-inch squares with a sharp knife. Place ¼ cup of ricotta cream in the center of each square, moisten the edges with a little water, and fold over to make a triangle. Press the edges with the tines of a fork to seal.

Put enough lard or oil to come to a depth of 3 inches into a large heavy-bottomed saucepan, and heat it to 375 degrees on a deep-fry or candy thermometer. Fry the *ravioli*, one at a time, for about 1 minute on each side, or until crispy and golden brown. Drain on paper towels and serve warm or at room temperature, dusted with powdered sugar.

MAKES 10

Honey Clusters
Pignolata

Pignolata show up all over Sicily under different names—*pagnuccata, pignoccata, pignolata*—from the word *pigna*, which means pinecone, the ancient fertility symbol that they resemble. In the eastern part of the island, *pignolata* are covered on one side with vanilla icing, on the other with chocolate. In the Aeolian Islands, off her north coast, they are called *giggi* and are glazed with a syrup of *vino cotto* instead of honey. In the United States, they are frequently called *struffoli* and they appear in pastry shops during Christmastime. This recipe comes from Piera Paolino, whose sister-in-law Angela gave me the recipe for the Saint Joseph's Day Fritters (*sfinci di San Giuseppe*) on page 135.

DOUGH

3 eggs

1 tablespoon sugar

¼ teaspoon salt

2 tablespoons vegetable oil

2¼ cups unbleached all-purpose flour, plus extra if needed

Vegetable oil for frying

SYRUP

¼ cup water

¼ cup sugar

1 teaspoon grated orange zest

1½ cups orange blossom honey

Colored candy sprinkles (diavolicchi)

For the Dough

In a large mixing bowl, beat the eggs lightly with a wooden spoon to blend, then beat in the sugar, salt, and oil. Sift in the flour and mix to form a soft, but not sticky, dough; add a bit more flour if the dough is sticky. Turn out onto a lightly floured work surface and knead for 5 minutes or so, until smooth. Cover and let rest for 30 minutes.

Divide the dough into 8 pieces and roll, one at a time, into ropes about ½ inch thick. With a sharp knife, cut each rope into ½-inch pieces, and transfer the pieces to a lightly floured baking sheet, separating them so they don't stick to one another. Cover loosely with a kitchen towel and let them rest while you heat the oil.

In a large, deep heavy saucepan, heat 3 inches of oil to 350 degrees on a deep-fry or candy thermometer. Fry a handful of the pieces of dough at a time in the hot oil, stirring with a wooden spoon so they brown evenly, until they are a deep golden brown, about 3 minutes. Drain on paper towels.

For the Syrup
In a large pot or deep frying pan, bring the water, sugar, and orange zest to a boil, stirring constantly until the sugar is dissolved. Stir in the honey. Reduce the heat to medium-high and add the little balls, stirring to coat them evenly with the syrup. (Please use caution when working with this syrup—it is hot, hot, hot.) Continue to cook and stir for 5 to 10 minutes, or until the balls have absorbed some of the syrup and look glazed; do not allow the syrup to get too dark. There may be some leftover syrup. Turn the balls of dough out onto a heat-proof platter and, using a metal spoon dipped in water, coax them into a pile that resembles a pinecone. Sprinkle immediately with the candy sprinkles.

M AKES 1 LARGE

Rice Fritters
Crispelle di Riso

These honey-drenched fritters were first prepared in the eighteenth century by the Benedictine brothers of San Nicola Monastery in Catania. They are now made for Saint Martin's Day on November 11 by pastry chefs, street vendors, and home cooks from Catania to Siracusa.

1½ cups milk, divided

1¼ cups water, divided

¼ teaspoon salt

One 3-inch cinnamon stick

Grated zest of 1 orange

1 cup short-grain rice, Arborio or Vialone preferred

2 teaspoons active dry yeast

1¼ cups unbleached all-purpose flour

Vegetable oil for frying

1 cup orange blossom honey

In a large saucepan with a tight-fitting lid, bring 1 cup of the milk, 1 cup of the water, the salt, cinnamon stick, and orange zest to a boil. Lower the heat, add the rice, stir, and simmer, covered, for 20 minutes, or until all the liquid is absorbed. Spread the rice out on a baking sheet, remove the cinnamon stick, and let cool, covered, overnight.

The next day, bring the rice to room temperature and transfer it to a large bowl. In a small saucepan, warm the remaining ½ cup milk to body temperature (it should feel neither hot nor cold when tested with a clean finger). Remove from the heat and dissolve the yeast in the warm milk. Allow to sit for 10 minutes, until the yeast is foamy. Add the milk-yeast mixture and flour to the rice and mix well. Cover and let rise in a warm place for 2 hours, or until the dough becomes puffy.

In a large deep heavy-bottomed saucepan, heat 3 inches of oil to 375 degrees on a deep-fry or candy thermometer. Spread half the dough out on a small wooden cutting board to form a rectangle roughly 3 inches by 10 inches. Holding the board above the oil, using a sharp knife (you can rest it on the edge of the pan), cut off ½-inch-wide strips of dough from a short side of the rectangle (so that each piece measures 1 inch by 3 inches) and scrape them with the knife into the oil; fry only a few at a time. Cook the *crispelle* for about 30 seconds on each side until golden, and drain them on paper towels. Keep the cooked fritters warm in a 250-degree oven while you fry the rest.

In a small saucepan, dilute the honey with the remaining ¼ cup water and warm it over low heat. Drizzle the *crispelle* with the honey mixture before serving.

MAKES ABOUT 2 DOZEN

Pastry Ribbons for Carnival
Chiacchiere

Preparations for February's Carnival begin about three months early in Siracusa. By late November, piles of these crispy pastry ribbons covered in drifts of powdered sugar are beginning to appear in the shops and outdoor stalls. The name *chiacchiere* means "little gossips," referring to the chatty "psst and cackle" sounds they make as they hit the hot oil.

1½ cups unbleached all-purpose flour

1 tablespoon sugar

½ teaspoon baking powder

¼ teaspoon salt

2 tablespoons lard or vegetable shortening, chilled

1 egg

3 tablespoons sweet wine, such as Marsala

Vegetable oil for frying

1 cup powdered sugar

Sift the flour, sugar, baking powder, and salt into a medium mixing bowl. Cut in the lard or shortening until the mixture resembles coarse cornmeal. In a small bowl, beat together the egg and wine to blend. Pour into the flour mixture and mix until the dough comes together in a ball.

(continued)

Turn the dough out onto a lightly floured work surface and knead for 5 minutes, or until smooth. Cover and refrigerate for 1 hour before rolling out.

Divide the chilled dough into 4 pieces. Keep the unused portion covered while you work. Roll a piece of the dough very, very thin, dusting the work surface with a tiny bit of flour if it sticks. You should be able to read a newspaper through the dough—I know this is expecting a lot from both the dough and the cook, but do the best you can while bearing in mind that the thinner the dough, the crispier and more delicate the cookies. Cut the dough into 2 by 4-inch strips using a fluted pastry wheel or a pizza cutting wheel.

In a large deep heavy saucepan, heat 3 inches of oil to 350 degrees on a deep-fry or candy thermometer. Fry the *chiacchiere,* a few at a time, turning once, until nicely browned, about 45 seconds per side. Drain the cookies on paper towels.

Place the powdered sugar in a paper bag and toss in a few *chiacchiere* at a time, shaking the bag to coat them with sugar.

MAKES ABOUT 5 DOZEN

Cannoli

The first thing that comes to mind when most people think of Sicilian sweets is the *cannolo* (plural: *cannoli*). The word *cannoli* means "pipes," and they are indeed pipes—of crispy pastry filled with one of several mixtures: ricotta cream (the most common), pastry cream, chocolate cream, or even pistachio cream.

It is likely that the first *cannoli* were filled with the tangy sheep's milk ricotta for which Sicily is justly famous and honey. In the tenth century, the Arabs added sugar, candied fruit, and cinnamon, and in the sixteenth century, with the chocolate brought to Sicily by the Spanish, *cannoli* became the pastries we know today.

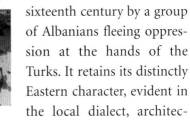

It was during this time that *cannoli* production began to take root in convent kitchens, most particularly around the time of Carnival, the rowdy festivities marking the beginning of Lent. Sicilian culinary historian Giuseppe Pitrè calls the *cannolo* the *corona del pranzo carnevalesco,* the crown of the carnival lunch. From their beginning, *cannoli* have maintained an association with rites of passage involving birth and rebirth. They are believed to have been fashioned after ancient stone columns, fertility symbols of the Greeks.

To understand traditional *cannoli,* you must first know ricotta.

The finest ricotta is thought to be made in the area around Piana degli Albanesi, a small mountain town about twenty-five miles south of Palermo. The town was settled in the sixteenth century by a group of Albanians fleeing oppression at the hands of the Turks. It retains its distinctly Eastern character, evident in the local dialect, architecture, and spectacular Byzantine rites performed in its Greek Orthodox churches, especially during Easter.

The ricotta from this area is made from the milk of sheep (or sometimes goats) who graze on fragrant mountain herbs. It produces a firm-bodied cheese, prized for its tangy, earthy flavor.

Early one morning at the open-air Vucciria Market in Palermo, a cheese vendor named Totò told us about a man named Salvatore who makes ricotta in a small shop on the main street of Piana degli Albanesi. In order to locate him, we would have to go to the Bar di Noto and ask for Lou. We got in the car and headed south.

Finding the Bar di Noto was easy. Extricating ourselves from the grip of Lou was not. He has some sort of vague proprietary interest in the bar and functions as a self-appointed curator of local history. Lou likes an audience, and that day, we were it.

I explained that I was writing a book and asked how to find Salvatore. "Siddown, you'll have some coffee first," he commanded in heavily accented English with an edge of Bensonhurst (and completely ignoring the Salvatore request). "You gotta contract for this book?" It was almost accusatory. "You gotta have a contract—I know a man down the street, he can make you the contract. Gotta have the contract."

"I have the contract. What I need is cheese. From Salvatore."

Lou was not about to be easily derailed. For the next two hours, he talked and we listened. He had lived in the United States for some time, hauling "goods." He never said what it was he hauled. Now here he was, in this secluded mountain town, "resting." I could see I'd have to beat him at his own game.

"So Lou. About this Salvatore. You must tell me where he is. If I don't find the ricotta, I can't write the book. If I can't write the book, I don't get the money. If I don't get the money, my children will starve." (I have no children.) "How will you feel, Lou, taking food out of my children's mouths?"

"Money? Bah! You gotta do the work for the love, not the money."

"What are you, Lou, some kinda Sicilian Buddha?" I asked.

"*Buddha?* Buddha bust you balls for the money!"

I'm pretty sure he was talking about a different Buddha.

"Okay, I tell you where to find this Salvatore, but you shoulda come two hours ago. He already finish makin' the cheese now!" We were told to go to the main street and look for the goat carcass.

The goat skin (not actually a carcass, thankfully) that hangs from a hook just outside Salvatore's shop is proof that no part of the goat, or sheep, is wasted here. After a few days in the hot Sicilian sun, the tanned skins are sold to a bootmaker in Milan.

Three generations of Salvatores work seven days a week making cheese, sausage, and salami. We arrived just as Papà Salvatore, with two inches of ash balanced precariously at the end of his cigarette, was scooping the last of the day's ricotta into its baskets to drain. His son Salvatore arrived shortly afterward with baby-food jars of sweet, hot espresso for us to drink while we tasted a batch of the day's ricotta, still warm and drizzled with honey.

Sicilian ricotta has a distinctive tang that's missing from the American variety, made of cow's milk. American supermarket ricotta is almost useless in cooking unless you drain it for several hours to remove the excess moisture. To do this, line a strainer or colander with a triple thickness of dampened cheesecloth, set it over a bowl, add the ricotta, and let it drain overnight in the refrigerator. Or make your own.

"Tell me, *signorina*. You have sheep in Newi Yorki? No? Then you cannot make the ricotta!"

You don't need to have sheep to make your own ricotta, it just won't be the same as what you'll find in Sicily. To add some tang to cow's milk ricotta, either homemade or store-bought, try combining it with a small amount of unflavored fresh goat cheese.

Like most Sicilians, the Salvatores use rennet, a by-product of sheep's stomach, to make their cheese. With respect to vegetarians, and those folks to whom rennet is not readily available, here is a way to make ricotta using vinegar:

Homemade Ricotta Cheese

3½ quarts whole milk

2 cups half-and-half

⅓ cup distilled white vinegar

4 ounces unflavored fresh goat cheese, optional

In a stainless-steel or enameled saucepan, whisk together the milk, half-and-half, and vinegar. Insert a candy thermometer into the pan making sure it doesn't touch the bottom of the pan. Over low heat, bring the mixture to 170 degrees, stirring occasionally to prevent sticking or scorching.

While the milk is heating, line a colander or strainer with a double thickness of damp cheesecloth or paper towels and place it over a large bowl.

As the milk mixture approaches 170 degrees, it will separate into solid curds and nearly clear liquid (whey). When this happens, immediately turn off the heat and scoop out the curds with a slotted spoon, transferring them to the prepared colander.

Allow the curds to drain and cool at room temperature for at least an hour. If you are adding goat cheese, blend it in now. Transfer to a 1-quart container and refrigerate, tightly covered, for up to 3 days.

M AKES ABOUT 1 QUART

To showcase their cheese-making prowess, the people of Piana degli Albanesi designed the *maxi cannoli*. It is the size of a fat forearm, bursting with a creamy mixture of sweetened ricotta, candied citron, and chocolate bits. The best place to sample it is Bar di Noto, where the ricotta is delivered, still warm, every morning. Lou presented us with a few before packing us off to Salvatore's.

Making our way into the center of town, we encountered a very slight, very feeble old widow, cloaked in black, inching her way up the steep hill with the aid of a rickety cane. I approached the little crone and offered up one of our *cannoli*. "What do you mean, *signorina*!" she barked, slashing the air in front of her with the cane. "Can't you see I have no teeth?" As I turned to make a sheepish but quick getaway, the end of her cane caught my hand like the rap of a nun's ruler. She gestured at the *cannoli*. "*Però, m'arrangio, signorina*" (I'll manage), she said as her gnarled hands reached for the *cannoli*.

When buying *cannoli* in Sicily, choose those that are filled to order, called *cannoli espressi* or *cannoli al momento*. Filling them too far in advance turns the normally crispy shell so soggy that it ruins everything. In Sicily, a special license is required to fill *cannoli* to order, since this is usually done in the shop rather than the *laboratorio*, governed by a different set of regulations. I would give anything to have been present at the meeting during which that issue was decided!

Cannoli have emigrated to the United States, though most of them lack the delicacy of their Sicilian cousins. This is due in great part to the excessive use of powdered sugar to stabilize the watery ricotta. Whether you decide to make your own ricotta or doctor up some store-bought ricotta, it's worth the effort; your *cannoli* will think they're in a little mountain town just south of Palermo.

SHELLS

1¾ cups unbleached all-purpose flour

2 tablespoons sugar

½ teaspoon cinnamon

¼ teaspoon salt

2 tablespoons lard or margarine, chilled and cut into ½-inch cubes

2 egg yolks

¼ to ½ cup sweet wine, such as Marsala

Lard or vegetable oil for frying

1 recipe Ricotta Cream (crema di ricotta; page 54)
    Chocolate Pastry Cream (crema di cioccolata; page 52),
    or Pistachio Pastry Cream (crema al pistacchio; page 51)

Powdered sugar for dusting

Chopped pistachios for garnish

Candied Orange Peel (scorzetta d'arancia candita; page 193)
    or halved candied cherries for garnish

Cannoli

For the Shells

Sift the flour, sugar, cinnamon, and salt into a large bowl. Make a well in the center and add the lard or margarine. Using a pastry blender or a knife, cut in the lard or margarine until the mixture has the consistency of coarse cornmeal.

In a small bowl, beat together the egg yolks and wine. Add to the flour, a tablespoon at a time, just until the dough begins to cling together. It should be lumpy.

Turn the dough out onto a lightly floured work surface and knead until it is smooth and satiny and tiny blisters appear on the surface. The blisters mean that the wine is beginning its fermentation in the dough, which will produce a crisp, light shell. Inadequate kneading will result in large, irregular air pockets in the dough that will puff up and explode when they hit the oil, taking your beautiful shells with them. Cover the dough and let it rest in a cool place for 1 hour.

On a floured surface, roll out the dough ¹⁄₁₆ inch thick and cut it into 3-inch circles with a glass or cookie cutter. With a rolling pin, roll the circles into 3 by 5-inch ovals.

Wrap each oval up around an aluminum *cannoli* tube (see Sources) and seal the edges with a little water. Meanwhile, in a deep heavy-bottomed saucepan, add enough lard or oil to come to a depth of 3 inches; heat to 350 degrees on a deep-fry or a candy thermometer. Fry 2 or 3 *cannoli* shells at a time (on their tubes) until golden brown and crispy, about 1½ minutes. Holding the *cannoli* tubes with tongs, gently shake the shells loose and drain them on paper towels. Let cool completely before filling.

Fill a large pastry bag with any one of the fillings and squeeze it into the shells, filling half of each shell at a time and working from the center out to the ends. Dust the cannoli with powdered sugar and decorate the ends with chopped pistachios and candied orange peel or cherries.

MAKES 16

T he Pasticceria Maria in the medieval town of Erice is mecca to anyone searching for the definitive almond pastry. The proprietress, Maria Grammatico, learned her craft from the sisters at the Convent of San Carlo in Erice while still a young girl, and she now owns and operates both a thriving *pasticceria* and a charming little tea salon.

Cream-Filled Doughnuts
Krapfen

Although her almond pastries and marzipan fruit are legendary (read about them in *Bitter Almonds,* written by Signora Grammatico and Mary Taylor Simeti), locals know to arrive here on Sunday, the only day she makes *krapfen*, at around noon, when the puffy, cream-filled pastries are still warm. Though their provenance is uncertain—some say a Frau Krapft fried up the first batch in the late 1600s—it's not surprising that Sicilians would embrace them so fully, given their love of *zeppole* and *sfinci,* close cousins.

2 cups water

8 tablespoons (1 stick) unsalted margarine

6 tablespoons sugar

1 teaspoon salt

1 teaspoon grated lemon zest

One ¼-ounce package active dry yeast

6 cups unbleached all-purpose flour

4 egg yolks, beaten lightly to blend

Vegetable oil for frying

1 recipe Pastry Cream (crema pasticciera; page 50)

Powdered sugar for dusting

In a small saucepan over medium heat, combine the water, margarine, sugar, salt, and lemon zest and heat until the margarine is melted. Let cool to lukewarm. Add the yeast to the cooled liquid and allow to sit for 5 minutes, or until the yeast dissolves and begins to foam.

Put the flour in a large bowl and make a well in the center. Pour the yeast mixture and the egg yolks into the well and stir with a wooden spoon, incorporating the flour a little at a time, until a rather soft but not sticky dough forms. Turn the dough out onto a lightly floured work surface and knead vigorously for 5 to 10 minutes, or until smooth and satiny. Put the dough in a greased bowl, cover the bowl tightly with plastic wrap, and allow to rise in a warm spot for 1½ hours, or until doubled in bulk.

Turn the dough out onto a lightly floured work surface and roll out ½ inch thick. Cut out rounds of dough with a floured 3-inch cookie cutter, then gather and reroll the scraps. Cover the rounds lightly with plastic wrap or a towel and let rise for 30 to 45 minutes, or until doubled once more.

Heat 3 inches of oil in a deep heavy saucepan until it reaches 350 degrees on a deep-fry or candy thermometer. Fry the *krapfen* in the hot oil, turning a few times, until puffy and well browned, about 2 minutes on each side. Remove and drain on paper towels. Let cool completely.

Split the cooled *krapfen* with a sharp knife about halfway through (like Pac-men) and fill with the pastry cream. Dust with powdered sugar and serve immediately.

Sweet Sicily

✳

MAKES ABOUT 1 DOZEN

S*finci* as we find them today were once made by the Sisters of the Convent of the Stigmata in Palermo to honor Saint Joseph, patron saint of pastry chefs. Made from the same dough as cream puffs (*bignè*), they are often baked instead of fried, and filled with pastry cream or whipped cream. This recipe was given to me by Angela Paolino, who lives in Pietraperzia.

Saint Joseph's Day Fritters

Sfinci di San Giuseppe

> 8 tablespoons (1 stick) unsalted butter or margarine,
>   cut into ½-inch cubes
>
> ¾ cup water
>
> 1 tablespoon sugar
>
> Pinch of salt
>
> 1 cup unbleached all-purpose flour
>
> Vegetable oil for frying
>
> 4 eggs
>
> 1 recipe Pastry Cream (crema pasticciera; page 50) or ½ cup warmed orange
>   blossom honey

In a medium heavy-bottomed saucepan, bring the butter or margarine, water, sugar, and salt to a boil, stirring with a wooden spoon until all the butter is melted. Remove from the heat and add the flour all at once, stirring with gusto until the dough forms a ball that pulls away from the sides of the pan. It will be sticky. Allow it to cool, stirring every now and then to release steam, for 15 minutes.

Meanwhile, heat 2 inches of oil in a heavy saucepan to 325 degrees on a deep-fry or candy thermometer.

Beat the eggs into the dough one at a time, making sure that each one is well incorporated before adding the next. The dough should be loose but not runny.

(continued)

Fried
Pastries

✹

135

To fry the *sfinci,* dip a tablespoon first in the hot oil (the oil will prevent the dough from sticking to the spoon), then scoop out a spoonful of dough and drop it into the oil. You can fry a few at a time, but don't crowd the pan. After about 1½ minutes, the dough will begin to brown and puff up. Turn it over, and an amazing thing will happen. The *sfinci* will pop open and puff up to about twice their size. This may happen slowly or all at once—each one is different. Continue to fry, turning the *sfinci* once or twice, until evenly browned. When they are done, drain them on paper towels.

If you are going to fill the *sfinci,* allow them to cool completely, then split them open and fill them with the pastry cream, using a large spoon (or see the recipe for *lulus* on page 112 for directions using a pastry bag). To serve the *sfinci* with honey, keep the fried *sfinci* warm on a platter in a 250-degree oven until they are all cooked, then drizzle them with honey and serve immediately.

MAKES ABOUT 2 DOZEN

Pumpkin Fritters
Sfinci di Cucuzza

In Lipari, one of the largest of the Aeolian Islands off the north coast of Sicily, there is a local custom similar to an American barn raising. Men of an entire neighborhood gather to lay the foundation of a home. Much merriment accompanies the mixing of cement, gravel, and water, and when it's time to take a break, the women arrive with bottles of wine and baskets of sweets. Whether or not a building is to survive depends on the quality (and quantity) of the sweets consumed at its raising. These fritters are always in the basket.

One 1-pound piece sugar pumpkin or winter squash,
    seeds removed

½ cup sugar, divided

¼ cup warm water

One ¼-ounce package active dry yeast

3 egg yolks

*2 teaspoons finely chopped fresh rosemary
    or 1 teaspoon crumbled dried rosemary*

¾ teaspoon salt

3½ cups unbleached all-purpose flour

1 teaspoon baking powder

½ cup dark raisins or currants

Vegetable oil for frying

Preheat the oven to 400 degrees.

Place the pumpkin or squash in a baking pan just large enough to hold it and pour 1 cup boiling water into the pan. Cover and bake for 45 minutes, or until very soft.

Scrape the pumpkin or squash flesh from the skin and push through a ricer or a food mill to remove all the membrane and any seeds. Measure out 1 cup of the puree and set aside.

Meanwhile, in a large bowl, add ¼ cup of the sugar to the warm water and sprinkle in the yeast. Allow the mixture to sit for 5 minutes, or until the yeast begins to foam. When the yeast is foamy, add the yolks, rosemary, pumpkin or squash puree, and salt, and stir to combine. Sift the flour with the baking powder and add to the mixture all at once, stirring vigorously until the mixture becomes a stiff batter (or a loose dough, depending on how you look at it). Stir in the raisins or currants, cover the bowl, and allow it to sit in a warm place for 1½ hours, or until the dough is doubled in bulk.

Heat 2 inches of oil in a large, heavy saucepan to 350 degrees on a deep-fry or candy thermometer. To fry the *sfinci,* dip a tablespoon into the hot oil, (the oil will prevent the *sfinci* from sticking to the spoon), scoop up a small spoonful of dough, and drop into the pot. You can cook a few at a time, but don't crowd them. It should take about a minute for them to brown on one side, when they are ready to flip over and brown for another minute. Sometimes they flip by themselves, sometimes you have to give them a little nudge with the spoon. Cook them for a total of about 2 minutes to brown evenly. Drain the *sfinci* on paper towels and sprinkle them with the remaining ¼ cup sugar to serve. Serve warm or at room temperature.

MAKES ABOUT 3 DOZEN

Doughnuts for Saint Joseph's Day

Zeppole

The *zeppole* is no stranger to the United States. If you've been to a street festival in any Little Italy in America, you know the *zeppole*, a kind of fried doughnut that is tossed in a bag with powdered sugar. In Sicily, *zeppole* are tiny and fluffy and rolled in granulated sugar. On many parts of the island, Saint Joseph's Day is celebrated on March 19 with solemn suppers given in gratitude to the saint for favors granted. Throughout Sicily, though, Saint Joseph is feted with street fairs and *zeppole*, and you must pull the ear of anyone you meet on this day named Giuseppe (Joseph) for good luck!

1½ cups milk

One ¼-ounce package active dry yeast

¼ cup sugar

Grated zest of 1 lemon

4½ cups unbleached all-purpose flour

1 teaspoon baking powder

¾ teaspoon salt

½ teaspoon cinnamon

Vegetable oil for frying

1 cup powdered or granulated sugar

In a small saucepan, heat the milk to body temperature (it should feel neither hot nor cold when tested with a clean finger). Remove from the heat, add the yeast and sugar, and let sit for 5 minutes, or until the yeast begins to foam. Add the lemon zest.

Sift together the flour, baking powder, salt, and cinnamon into a large mixing bowl. Add the yeast mixture and stir vigorously until the dough comes together. Turn the dough out onto a lightly floured work surface and knead it with gusto for about 10 minutes, or until it is smooth and satiny, like a baby's bottom. Cover and let rise in a warm place until doubled in bulk, 1 to 1½ hours.

When the dough has risen, heat 2 inches of oil in a large heavy saucepan to 350 degrees on a deep-fry or candy thermometer. Grab a handful of dough and squeeze it gently so some of it pops out the side of your fist between your thumb and forefinger. When you have a piece the size of a walnut, squeeze your thumb and forefinger together to release the ball of dough into the hot oil. (Or follow the frying directions for the Pumpkin Fritters on page 136.) Fry the *zeppole*, a few at a time, for about 1½ minutes on each side, or until browned on both sides, then transfer them with a slotted spoon to paper towels to drain.

Put the powdered or granulated sugar in a paper bag and drop a few *zeppole* at a time into the bag, shaking to coat with the sugar.

Makes about 2 dozen

Cakes

Torte

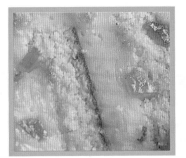

$\mathcal{M}$y invitation to the thousandth birthday party of the *cassata* must have gotten lost in the mail. Otherwise I would have been in Palermo in 1998 to have my taste of the 1,000-kilo *cassata* that pastry chefs from all over the island joined forces to create. It is a measure of the high esteem with which Sicilians regard their pastry that they would pull out all the stops for a *cake*.

Perhaps more than any other pastry, the *cassata* reveals centuries of Sicilian history in its components: Greek ricotta; Spanish sponge cake, chocolate, and candied squash; and Saracen sugar, citrus fruit, and almond paste.

Sicilian food historian Pino Correnti believes that the *cassata* was born in Palermo during Arab rule in the year 998. The name *cassata* in fact comes from the Arabic *q'as at*, meaning "box"—the

Opposite: Cassata, page 150

box in this case being a round pan with sloping sides in which the *cassata* is traditionally made.

Rarely will you find Sicilian cakes being made in the home. Their place is in the *pasticcerie,* and even the convents, where as early as the sixteenth century nuns were outdoing pastry chefs in the sophistication of their creations.

There is the story of a sixteenth-century bishop in Mazara del Vallo, who, noticing a marked decline in attendance at his sermons, forbade the production of *cassata* during the Easter season. Thus he was assured of the nuns' devotions to their prayers rather than their ovens.

Triumph of Gluttony
Trionfo di Gola

In the sixteenth and seventeenth centuries, the decadent taste buds of Sicily's aristocracy were catered to by cloistered nuns baking in convent kitchens. Judging by the works of edible excess they turned out, it would seem that all mortal and carnal desire found its expression in their pastry—and none was more excessive than the "triumph of gluttony." The Convent of the Origlione in Palermo was home to the first triumph of gluttony, and other convents soon followed suit.

With three days' notice, the sisters at the Badia Santo Spirito in Agrigento will make a triumph of gluttony that serves about ten.

1 recipe Sponge Cake batter (pan di Spagna; page 58)

⅓ recipe Sweet Pastry Dough (pasta frolla; page 62)

*½ cup Squash Preserves (zuccata; page 190) or diced Candied Orange Peel
   (scorzetta d'arancia candita; page 193)*

½ recipe Milk Pudding (biancomangiare; page 174), chilled and set

2 cups Pistachio Preserves (conserva di pistacchi; page 188)

6 tablespoons Tangerine Liqueur (mandarinetto; page 199) or orange liqueur

½ recipe Marzipan (pasta reale; page 61), tinted green or pink if desired

Marzipan or sugar roses and gold dragées for decoration

Preheat the oven to 350 degrees.

Bake the sponge cake batter as directed in one 6-inch round pan, one 7-inch round pan, and one 8-inch round pan. You will have 3 thin layers. Increase the oven temperature to 375 degrees.

Press the pastry dough into the bottom only of a 9-inch fluted tart pan with a removable bottom and bake until browned. Let cool, then remove from the pan and transfer to a serving plate.

Stir the squash preserves or orange peel into the milk pudding.

To Assemble the Cake

Spread a thin layer of pistachio preserves on the baked pastry crust, to within ½ inch of the edges. Place the 8-inch cake layer over it and sprinkle with 2 tablespoons of the liqueur. Spread another thin layer of the pistachio preserves on the cake and follow with half of the milk pudding mixture. Place the 7-inch layer on top, sprinkle it with 2 tablespoons liqueur, and spread a thin layer of preserves over it. Top with the remaining pudding mixture and then the 6-inch layer. Sprinkle with the remaining 2 tablespoons liqueur and spread a thin layer of preserves over it. Cover the cake with plastic wrap and refrigerate for at least 2 hours.

Unwrap the cake and trim the sides to smooth out the "steps," leaving a dome shape. Spread the remaining pistachio preserves carefully over the top and sides of the cake, covering it completely.

Roll out the marzipan between two sheets of waxed paper into a 14-inch circle and drape it over the top and sides of the cake. Press it so it adheres smoothly. Decorate with marzipan or sugar roses and gold dragées, or anything else that suits your fancy. After all, it is a triumph of gluttony!

Makes 12 to 14 servings

Tangerine Cake
Torta al Mandarino

I f I lived in Ragusa, I'd order this birthday cake every year from the Pasticceria di Pasquale.

1 recipe Sponge Cake (pan di Spagna; page 58)

1 recipe Pastry Cream (crema pasticciera; page 50)

1 tablespoon grated tangerine zest

6 tablespoons Tangerine Liqueur (mandarinetto; page 199) or orange liqueur

GLAZE

⅓ cup heavy whipping cream

½ teaspoon vanilla

2 teaspoons grated tangerine zest

6 cups powdered sugar, sifted

A few drops orange food coloring, optional

Line a 10-inch springform pan with plastic wrap. Cut the sponge cake into three ½-inch layers. Combine the pastry cream and tangerine zest.

Place 1 cake layer in the bottom of the prepared pan, sprinkle with 2 tablespoons of the tangerine liqueur, and spread with half the pastry cream. Repeat with another layer of cake, 2 more tablespoons of the liqueur, and the remaining pastry cream. Finish with the final cake layer and the remaining liqueur. Chill, covered, for at least 3 hours, or overnight.

For the Glaze
Whisk together all the ingredients until smooth. Keep tightly covered until ready to use.

Invert the cake onto a serving dish and remove the pan and plastic wrap. Spread the glaze evenly over the top and sides of the cake with a metal spatula. Let the glaze set for 30 minutes before serving.

MAKES 10 TO 12 SERVINGS

Chocolate-Hazelnut Cake

Torta Savoia

The Courtship of Sweet Sicily lasted only three years (1713–1716) under the Duke of Savoy. Though his reign was forgettable, he is remembered in this cake that so regally bears his name.

SYRUP

> ½ cup sugar
>
> ½ cup water
>
> 6 tablespoons dark rum

FILLING

> One 13-ounce jar Nutella (chocolate-hazelnut cream)
>
> 1½ cups heavy whipping cream, divided
>
> 1 teaspoon vanilla
>
> 1 recipe Sponge Cake (pan di Spagna; page 58)

GLAZE

> 1 cup heavy whipping cream
>
> 2 tablespoons unsalted butter, at room temperature
>
> 12 ounces semisweet chocolate, chopped

For the Syrup

Combine the sugar and water in a small saucepan, bring to a boil, and boil until the sugar is dissolved and the mixture is reduced by one-quarter. Let cool, and stir in the rum.

For the Filling

In a small bowl, whisk the Nutella with ½ cup of the cream to lighten the Nutella. In a mixing bowl, whip the remaining 1 cup cream with the vanilla until it begins to hold its shape. Add the Nutella mixture and continue to whip until stiff.

To Assemble the Cake

Line a 10-inch springform pan with plastic wrap. Cut the sponge cake into three ½-inch layers. Place 1 cake layer in the bottom of the pan, brush with one-third of the rum syrup, and spread evenly with half the filling. Repeat with another layer of cake, another one-third syrup, and the remaining filling. Finish with the final cake layer and the remaining syrup. Chill, covered, for 2 hours before unmolding.

Meanwhile, Make the Glaze

Bring the cream and butter just to a boil and immediately remove from the heat. Add the chocolate and let sit for 5 minutes to allow the chocolate to melt, then whisk until smooth. This glaze solidifies significantly upon cooling; if it becomes too stiff to work with, warm it over low heat, stirring carefully.

Invert the cake onto a serving platter and remove the pan and plastic wrap. Pour or spread the glaze evenly over the top and sides of the cake. Allow the glaze to set before serving.

MAKES 12 TO 14 SERVINGS

Pasticceria Marciante

ORTIGIA, SIRACUSA

Corinthian Greeks who settled on the island of Ortigia colonized Siracusa in the eighth century B.C. Crossing over to Ortigia from Siracusa proper by way of a short footbridge means stepping back in time over two thousand years to Sicily's first Golden Age. We had arranged to visit the Pasticceria Marciante, located just off the main *piazza*. Arriving early (a first), we decided to have an espresso and check out the *duomo* (cathedral).

At first glance, it appears designed in the High Baroque style of the seventeenth century, but larger. Its scale is gargantuan, as are those of the surrounding buildings. Great hulking Corinthian columns support its mass, and a group of rather surly limestone poets gesture angrily from its

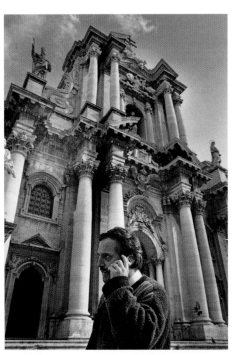

façade. Everything seems eerily disproportionate.

We discovered that this was originally a temple raised in honor of the goddess Athena in the fifth century B.C. In a seventh-century fit of adaptive reuse, walls were built connecting the columns, and the resulting edifice was consecrated as a Christian church. After the earthquake of 1693 destroyed its façade, Palermo architect Andrea Palma redesigned it in the Baroque style. It looks a little bloated.

Add to that the Fascist-era signage, Nazi propaganda posters, and even a quote from Mussolini (signed by Il Duce himself) that still appear freshly painted on an otherwise grimy wall, and what you have is a weirdly art-directed piazza. Was Fascism so great that the citizens of

Siracusa wanted to hang on to it forever? And hadn't anyone ever heard of *soap and water*?

That led to a very deep discussion among us California natives. Growing up in Los Angeles gives you a warped sense of reality: you look at everything as though it was a movie set. Now we were in the presence of *true history* and needed to develop some appreciation for the visual discord. How narrow-minded we had been. Where five minutes ago the walls had been sooty, they now had *patina*. It became obvious that Siracusa was a city that embraced—and displayed—every bit of its history.

It was decided that after our visit to the Marciantes we would explore further.

The brothers Marciante—Giuseppe and Valerio—are heirs to a pastry dynasty that goes back more than a century. The only *pasticceria* in Sicily to hold a Royal Warrant from Queen Elizabeth II, these men are as humble as they are talented. So accustomed are they to working together that they seem to be engaged in a continual *pas de deux* around the kitchen. They are quick to credit Papà Ernesto and Uncle Luigi for teaching them what they know about pastries and fraternal harmony.

They are, on both counts, blessed.

Would we like to try their *cassata*? The brothers had contributed their talents to help create a 1,000-kilogram *cassata* for its thousandth birthday party in Palermo in 1998 and are considered to be authorities on the art. Who could refuse such an offer? The *cassata* was scrumptious. The tiny jewellike candied

pears actually tasted like pears. The *cassata* at the Pasticceria Marciante comes in two sizes: 9-inch rounds and 3-inch miniatures. The brothers explained that under normal circumstances miniature *cassata*s are called *cassatine,* but theirs have a pert little cherry on top, thus qualifying them for the name—both

rushing to be the first to blurt it out—*virgin's breasts!* We were not as shocked as they thought we'd be.

Now that we'd seen the breasts, did we want to taste Saint Lucy's eyes? They blinked dramatically. The eyes in this case are an invention of Papà Ernesto—almond-shaped cookies with orange peel eyeballs, sold in pairs to honor the patroness of Siracusa, Santa Lucia.

Next we watched as the brothers handpainted dozens of marzipan fruits, working together with remarkable deftness and speed. Just to see what response I'd get, I asked if they'd ever consider airbrushing the fruits. "That would be an *americanata*." (*Americanata* is not a complimentary term; it denotes cheapness.) I said I knew they wouldn't dare.

Eager to get back to the *piazza,* we decided to accept the brothers' offer of breasts-to-go. We would photograph them in front of the gloomy, Fascist *duomo* to prove to ourselves how appreciative we really were of the city's *true history*.

In a fine example of the Sicilian way in which art-imitates-life-imitates-art, the brothers expressed horror at this idea: "But *signorina,* the piazza is not *normale.* It looks so gray and Fascist. You should come back after Signor Tornatore finishes making his film!"

Cassata

Syrup

> ½ cup sugar
>
> ½ cup water
>
> ¼ cup Strega or maraschino liqueur
>
> Green food coloring
>
> ½ recipe Marzipan (pasta reale; page 61)
>
> 1 recipe Sponge Cake (pan di Spagna; page 58)
>
> 1 recipe Ricotta Cream (crema di ricotta; page 54)
>
> ½ recipe (1½ cups) Lemon Icing (glassa di limone; page 57)
>
> Candied fruits for garnish

Line a 10-inch by 3-inch-deep round cake pan with sloping sides (see Sources) with plastic wrap, or use a springform pan.

For the Syrup
Combine the sugar and water in a small saucepan, bring to a boil, and boil until the sugar is dissolved and the mixture is reduced by one-quarter. Let cool, and stir in the liqueur.

Opposite: Cassata, *from the Caffè Sicilia, Noto*

To Assemble the Cake

Work enough food coloring into the marzipan to obtain a mint-green color. Roll it out between sheets of waxed paper or plastic wrap to make a 3-inch-wide strip that is long enough to line the sides of the cake pan. Fit the marzipan strip into the inside of the pan.

Cut the sponge cake crosswise into ½-inch-wide strips. Line the bottom of the pan with some of the strips, trimming them to fit. Brush the cake with half of the syrup. Spread the ricotta cream evenly on top of the cake; it should come to no more than ½ inch from the top of the pan, to leave room for another layer of cake. Cover the cream with a layer of cake strips that reaches all the way to the edges of the marzipan, trimming the strips to fit it. Brush with the remaining syrup. Cover the *cassata* with plastic wrap and refrigerate for at least 4 hours, or overnight.

Invert the cake onto a serving plate and remove the pan and plastic wrap. Pour the lemon icing over the top (and down the sides, if you wish) of the cake, spreading it evenly with a metal spatula. Decorate the top with candied fruits (don't hold back). The *cassata* will keep tightly covered in the refrigerator for up to 1 week.

MAKES 10 TO 12 SERVINGS

Fig-Filled Christmas Pastry Ring
Buccellato

You know that Christmas is coming when these fruit-filled pastry rings (their name means "bracelet") begin to appear in the pastry shops of Palermo. Clues to centuries of foreign domination on Sicilian shores are evident in the spicy complexity of their filling—figs and walnuts from the Greeks, cooked grape must syrup (*vino cotto*) from the Romans, lemons from the Arabs, and chocolate from the Spanish. Home cooks use the same ingredients to make *cucciddati*—chubby little pastries decorated with colored sprinkles that are enjoyed by families all throughout the Christmas season.

1 pound dried figs

½ cup golden raisins

½ cup walnuts, toasted

½ cup almonds, toasted

1 teaspoon cinnamon

½ teaspoon ground cloves

2 ounces semisweet chocolate, melted

¼ cup apricot jam

⅓ cup honey

⅓ cup Cooked Grape Must Syrup (vino cotto; page 202) or sweet Marsala

2 teaspoons grated lemon zest

½ recipe Sweet Pastry Dough (pasta frolla; page 62)

½ recipe (1½ cups) Sugar Icing (glassa di zucchero; page 55)

Colored candy sprinkles (diavolicchi)

Chopped pistachios

Cover the figs with boiling water and let sit for 10 minutes to plump. Drain.

Transfer the figs, raisins, and nuts to a food processor fitted with the steel blade and coarsely chop. Add the cinnamon, cloves, chocolate, jam, honey, *vino cotto* or Marsala, and zest and process until smooth.

Roll out the pastry dough into a thin rectangle 4 inches by 15 inches. Spread the fig mixture down the center of the dough and fold over the sides to enclose the filling, overlapping the edges slightly. Pinch the edges together to seal. Turn the dough seam side down and, with a sharp knife or clean scissors, make a series of decorative slashes about ½ inch apart all down the length of the roll. Join the ends to form a ring and transfer to a lightly greased baking sheet. Refrigerate for 15 minutes.

Preheat the oven to 425 degrees.

Bake the *buccellato* for 15 minutes, then turn the oven temperature down to 350 degrees and bake for another 15 to 20 minutes, or until deep golden brown. Let cool for 30 minutes.

Brush the *buccellato* with the sugar icing. While the icing is still wet, decorate it with colored sprinkles and chopped pistachios.

MAKES 10 TO 12 SERVINGS

Frozen Desserts

Gelati

"O si po o nun si po; ppi lu gilatu di San Calo'!"

"If we can or if we can't [afford to], we buy the ice cream of San Calogero!"

Frozen desserts have been made in Sicily since the Romans ran relays across the island, bringing snow from Mount Etna to freeze their custards. The ancient Greeks diluted honey and wine with floral waters and preserved the mixtures within the snow of Mount Etna to slake their thirst during the blazing summer months. In the Roman cookbook by Apicius, the term *sorbitio* means any drink, potion, or broth. It seems likely that this is the root of the word *sorbetto*, a frozen fruit dessert first concocted by the Arabs with citrus juice and Etna's snow. They called it *sharbat*. Frozen desserts are so integral to Sicilian life that there is even a verb used solely to describe eating them—*sorbire*. During the summer, Sicilians may start the day with *gelato* stuffed into a soft, sweet bun—a sort of Mediterranean ice cream sandwich!

Gelato is similar to American ice cream, but it is traditionally made with a base of *crema rinforzata*—really just a soupy milk pudding (*biancomangiare*) thickened with wheat starch. The starch serves to emulsify the finished dessert, creating a rich *gelato* without the fat of cream and eggs. The word *gelato* also refers to any and all frozen desserts, including *granita, schiumone,* and *pezzi duri* ("frozen pieces"), multiflavored ice cream molds. *Cassata gelata* is the most renowned of these, a frozen version of the beloved *cassata.*

The *fantasia* (pronounced "fahn-tah-zee-a") aspect of Sicilian cuisine finds its most flamboyant expression in *gelati.* Anything that can be scooped into a large, footed bowl and festooned with fruits, cream, paper umbrellas, crispy rolled cookies, and brightly colored plastic spoons is called a *coppa fantasia.* A one-scooper in a small paper dish is called a *coppetta,* and an *affogato* is a scoop of vanilla gelato "drowned" in hot espresso.

Lemon Ice
Granita al Limone

The lemon groves in the fertile valley near Palermo called the Conca d'Oro were planted over a thousand years ago by Arab farmers, and there they grow today. Sicilians will tell you it's the hot Mediterranean sun that makes their lemons sing, or maybe it's the soil. In any case, Sicilians love their lemons. You can spot a Sicilian by the way they eat one. A true Siculo sprinkles it with salt and eats it plain. Just like that. During the summer, a typical Sicilian breakfast consists of lemon *granita* (or *gelato*) piled into a soft, sweet bun called a *brioscia* and eaten out of hand. I can't think of anything better than strolling down to the beach in Lipari on a summer morning with my lemon *granita* from Bar Oscar.

> *1½ cups sugar*
> *4 cups water*
> *Grated zest of 3 lemons*
> *¾ cup freshly squeezed lemon juice (from 4 to 6 lemons)*

Have ready a 9 by 13-inch nonreactive metal pan.

In a medium saucepan, stir together the sugar, water, and zest and bring to a boil, stirring constantly until the sugar is dissolved. Remove from the heat and let cool completely.

Add the lemon juice to the sugar syrup and pour it into the metal pan. Freeze for 30 minutes, or until ice crystals begin to form around the edges of the pan. With a fork, stir the crystals back into the liquid and return the pan to the freezer. Repeat every 20 minutes or so until the *granita* is completely frozen and slushy. This should take about 2 hours.

MAKES ABOUT 1 QUART

Coffee Ice
Granita al Caffè

One of the first things the Arabs brought to Sicily was coffee, and their passion for drinking it. The coffee came from Yemen, a small country in the Middle East, and when the Arabs found it could be mixed with the snow from Mount Etna, *granita al caffè* was born.

1 cup sugar
2½ cups water
1 cup freshly brewed espresso
Sweetened whipped cream for garnish

Have ready a 9 by 13-inch metal pan.

In a medium saucepan, stir together the sugar and water and bring to a boil over medium heat, stirring constantly until the sugar is dissolved. Remove from the heat, stir in the espresso, and let cool completely.

Pour into the metal pan and freeze for 30 minutes, or until ice crystals begin to form around the edges of the pan. With a fork, stir the crystals back into the liquid and return the pan to the freezer. Repeat every 20 minutes or so until the *granita is* completely frozen and slushy. This should take about 2 hours. Serve the *granita* in individual cups garnished with a dollop of whipped cream.

MAKES ABOUT 1 QUART

Corrado Costanzo

BAKING AT THE RIGHT HAND OF GOD IN NOTO

"You're going to Noto? Well, then you must go see Corrado." I was in my friend Mary Kay Hartley's office at the Italian Government Tourist Board in New York rooting through her files for information on pastry shops. Mary Kay knows all the good places to go in Sicily, so I noted her friend Corrado's address and wrote him, asking if I could visit his shop and learn some of his secrets. He responded:

> *Dear Signora,*
>
> *I would be most honored to meet you in person and from me you will have the maximum collaboration. Together we will decide which of my recipes are of the most interest to you . . . every one of my pastries, every* gelato, *every* granita, *is the result of the union of simple, genuine ingredients. But my secret ingredient is the love I put in each of my creations.*
>
> > *Best regards,*
> > *Corrado Costanzo*

Corrado Costanzo was born in the Baroque city of Noto in 1929. The death of his father forced him into the working world at age eight, to apprentice at the knee of master pastry chef Francesco Fichera.

Upon the *maestro's* death in 1962, his young protégé opened a shop of his own, located on an unassuming little side street just steps from the cathedral.

One of my photographer friend Tom's cameras was low on power, so before our three-hour drive we stopped to buy batteries. In the course of chatting up the shopgirls, Tom revealed our destination. *"Andate a Noto? Allora dovete andare a trovare Corrado!"* (You're going to Noto? Then you must go visit Corrado!)

We are a little bit behind schedule when Corrado himself receives us, all spit-and-polish clean, wearing a blindingly white apron. We offer handshakes but receive hugs. "You are late! I was expecting you twenty minutes ago." He tells us he's a Virgo. "Well, never mind, you're here now. Try some *cannoli*."

A half-dozen *cannoli*, some filled with chocolate, hit the table and, oh god, we still have such a *cannoli* hangover from the last two places we'd been.

"Thank you, *maestro,* but is there something you make that is unique to your shop?"

"Yes. Everything. These hands that make the *dolci*—they are *mani sapienti,* knowledgeable hands. Now try the *cannoli.*"

He scoffs at the title *maestro,* insisting that we call him, simply, Corrado. However, nobody deserves the title more than Corrado, on whom the president of the Italian Republic bestowed the honor *Cavaliere al Merito,* a distinction that is given to Italians whose work earns them a standing as ambassadors of culture and goodwill to all the world. He demonstrates his art and exhibits his work throughout Italy and Europe. His masterpieces in marzipan have twice been shown at the American Craft Museum in New York. But he is modest about his accomplishments, and this information comes only with some coaxing from his daughter Giusy (pronounced "juicy").

We eat the *cannoli* and taste the *amore.* Giusy, who works closely with her father, leads us into the *laboratorio.*

"Now you must try some of my father's *gelato.*"

It is difficult to focus on anything else after that. Jasmine *gelato* so redolent of the perfume of freshly picked blossoms it makes your heart sing.

"My father picks the flowers himself, in the evening, just as they begin to open."

We are in raptures over the rose petal *gelato*, tasting as you would imagine a love poem to. And the tangerine? It does a little *tarantella* on your palate. This man is picky about his ingredients, and it shows. I wanted to know everything.

"You already know about the history of this island, yes, *signorina*?"

"Yes, I do."

"And about how the Arabs brought the sugarcane and oranges, *eccetera, eccetera*?"

"Yes . . ."

"And the blessed sisters who baked in the convents?"

"Yesss . . ."

"Now I will tell you everything, *signorina*. *Primo*. You must have a love for your work, or—better said—you must work for love. It must be here [touching his heart] and here, in your hands. This you cannot learn. It is a gift from God. *Secondo*. You must know your ingredients. Nothing fancy, you understand, just simple. You must be sure they are genuine. Mine are pure Sicilian, grown in Sicilian soil. And, *terzo*. Work hard and be honest to yourself and to your art. And that's it. [Turning to Tom] Is that a Leica lens you are using? They are the best; the one

Cartier Bresson used. I am an aficionado of Cartier Bresson. Don't you think he is the master? Now there is an artist. There is a man who loved his work. Let's go back into the shop, where I will show you another work of art."

It seems an artist friend of Corrado's had wanted to present him with a mural painted just for his shop. The ever-popular Last Supper was chosen as the subject and executed whimsically. With one small alteration. Saint Peter has been replaced by Corrado, standing proudly in his dress whites and chef's hat, at the right hand of God. And that's exactly where he belongs.

When you go to Noto, you *must* go to see Corrado.

Tangerine Sorbet
Sorbetto al Mandarino

Nothing can come close to the transcendent tangerine *sorbetto* made by Corrado Costanzo in Noto. With this recipe I don't presume to duplicate his magic—you would need Sicilian tangerines, Sicilian water, Sicilian sun, and the passion of the *maestro* himself—but give it a try and let yourself dream.

1 cup sugar

1 cup water

Grated zest of 4 tangerines

3 cups tangerine juice (from 6 to 8 tangerines)

Juice of 1 lemon

Have ready a 9 by 13-inch nonreactive metal pan.

In a medium saucepan, stir together the sugar, water, and zest and bring to a boil, stirring constantly until the sugar is dissolved. Remove from the heat and let cool completely.

Strain the sugar syrup to remove the zest. Add the citrus juices and chill in the refrigerator for at least 1 hour.

Freeze in an ice cream freezer according to the manufacturer's directions.

MAKES ABOUT 1 QUART

Almond Milk Sherbet
Cremolata di Mandorla

In the eastern part of Sicily, *gelato* is frequently called *cremolata,* most often when it refers to *cremolata di mandorla.* At the Gelateria Costarelli in Acireale, the *cremolata* is made from the almonds of trees that have borne fruit since the Greeks landed on the island more than two thousand years ago, not ten miles away, in Naxos. During the hot summer months, it is often piled into a soft, sweet bun and eaten for breakfast.

½ recipe Almond Syrup (orzata; page 205) or 1½ cups store-bought almond syrup (see Sources)

4 cups water

In a bowl, stir together the almond syrup and water. Refrigerate until well chilled.

Freeze in an ice cream freezer according to the manufacturer's directions.

MAKES ABOUT 1 QUART

T rapani is a city on the west coast of Sicily that retains its distinctly Asian flavor. Jasmine is as beloved by the people of Trapani as it was when the Arabs first planted it on Sicilian soil over a thousand years ago. Its intoxicating aroma is distilled into jasmine water, which, in turn, is used to make this most ravishing *gelato*. One spoonful of the *scurzunera* from the Pasticceria Colicchia in Trapani and you'll imagine yourself languishing in the Gardens of Paradise.

Jasmine Gelato
Scurzunera

4 cups Jasmine Water (acqua di gelsomino; page 63)

1 cup sugar

One 3-inch cinnamon stick, broken

Juice of 1 small lemon

In a large saucepan, bring 1 cup of the jasmine water, the sugar, and cinnamon stick to a boil over medium heat, stirring until the sugar is dissolved. Remove from the heat and let cool completely. Remove the cinnamon, add the remaining 3 cups jasmine water and the lemon juice and refrigerate until chilled.

Freeze in an ice cream freezer according to the manufacturer's directions.

MAKES ABOUT 1 QUART

Ricotta Ice Cream
Gelato di Ricotta

At the Gelateria Costarelli in Acireale, the use of sheep's milk ricotta in the *gelato di ricotta* saves it from excessive sweetness. It has a mild tang and a pleasantly grainy texture, with just a whiff of cinnamon. Since sheep's milk ricotta is not readily available in this country, I have taken liberties with the recipe by adding a strip of lemon zest to give it the proper tang. Omit the lemon zest if you use any of the ricotta options discussed on page 128.

> 3 tablespoons cornstarch
>
> 3 cups milk, divided
>
> 1 cup sugar
>
> 1 strip lemon zest
>
> One 3-inch cinnamon stick, broken
>
> 1 cup whole-milk ricotta, well drained (see page 128)

Dissolve the cornstarch in ¼ cup of the milk and set aside.

Combine the remaining 2¾ cups milk, the sugar, lemon zest, and cinnamon stick in a large saucepan. Stir to dissolve the sugar and bring to a boil over medium heat. Whisk in the dissolved cornstarch and continue to cook until thickened. Strain to remove the lemon zest and cinnamon stick and let cool completely. Refrigerate until chilled.

Combine the ricotta with the chilled custard and freeze in an ice cream freezer according to the manufacturer's directions.

MAKES ABOUT 1½ QUARTS

This is the *nonno* (grandfather) of *spumoni*, created at the Gelateria Costarelli in Acireale. Popular through-out the island, *schiumone* is also known as *torrone gelato* (frozen nougat) in Catania, as it closely resembles the egg-white-based, almond-studded candy of that name.

2 egg whites

½ cup sugar

1 cup heavy whipping cream

2 teaspoons vanilla

1 cup almonds, toasted and chopped

Line six 3-inch muffin or custard cups with paper cupcake liners.

In the top of a double boiler or a stainless-steel mixing bowl set over a pot of simmer-ing water (do not let the water touch the bottom of the bowl), whisk together the egg whites and sugar. Continue to whisk gently until the sugar is dissolved and the mixture is warm to the touch (test it with a clean finger). Remove from the heat and, with an electric mixer on medium-high speed, beat the mixture until white and fluffy and com-pletely cool.

In a medium bowl, combine the cream and vanilla and, with the same beaters, whip until soft peaks form. Fold the whipped cream into the beaten egg whites until com-pletely incorporated, then fold in the almonds. Spoon the *schiumone* into the prepared cups and freeze for at least 3 hours.

MAKES 6 SERVINGS

Frozen Cassata

Cassata Gelata

This dessert belongs to the family of ice creams known as *pezzi duri*, literally, hard pieces, referring to their being made in molds and served in slices rather than scooped. *Cassata gelata* is an elaborate ice cream cake, even by Sicilian standards, and bears more than a passing resemblance to the multicolored *spumoni* served in Italian-American restaurants.

During the summer, stop by Antico Chiosco in Mondello Beach just outside Palermo and take a slice of their *cassata gelata* along on your sultry evening *passeggiata*.

1 recipe Sponge Cake (pan di Spagna; page 58)

6 tablespoons light or dark rum

1 pint best-quality vanilla ice cream

1 pint best-quality pistachio ice cream

1 pint best-quality chocolate ice cream

1 recipe Frozen Vanilla Mousse (schiumone; page 165),
    prepared to the point of freezing

¼ cup diced candied fruit, divided

¼ cup semisweet chocolate chips, divided

Cut the sponge cake into two ¾-inch-thick layers (reserve any remaining cake for another use).

Line the bottom of a 10-inch springform pan with a circle of waxed paper cut to fit. Place 1 cake layer in the pan and sprinkle it with 3 tablespoons of the rum. Let the vanilla ice cream soften slightly, then spread it evenly over the cake in the pan. Place in the freezer to firm.

Meanwhile, let the pistachio ice cream soften slightly. When the vanilla layer has hardened sufficiently, spread the pistachio ice cream evenly on top. Cover with the second cake layer and sprinkle with the remaining 3 tablespoons rum. Return to the freezer for 30 minutes.

Let the chocolate ice cream soften slightly. Spread it on top of the cake layer and return it to the freezer.

Prepare the frozen vanilla mousse as directed, folding in half the candied fruit and half the chocolate chips with the cream. Pile this on top of the chocolate ice cream layer and top with the remaining candied fruit and chocolate. Freeze for at least 3 hours before serving.

To unmold, dip a kitchen towel in very hot water, wring it out, and wrap it around the outside of the springform pan for a minute or so. Run a small knife around the inside of the pan if the *cassata* is stubborn. Remove the sides of the pan. You should be able to coax the *cassata* off its waxed paper–covered bottom with a spatula and very little effort.

MAKES 12 TO 14 SERVINGS

Spoon Sweets

Dolci al Cucchiaio

A t the end of the meal appeared a rum jelly. This was the Prince's favorite pudding, and the Princess had been careful to order it early that morning in gratitude for favors granted. It was rather threatening at first sight, shaped like a tower with bastions and battlements and smooth slippery walls impossible to scale, garrisoned by red and green cherries and pistachio nuts; but into its transparent and quivering flanks a spoon plunged with astounding ease.

—*The Leopard*, Giuseppe Tomasi di Lampedusa

Opposite: Lemon Pudding, page 170

Lemon Pudding

Budino di Limone

Sicilian lemons are legendary. No other lemon has the intensity of flavor or spiciness of a lemon from the Island in the Sun. That's why using just the zest for this pudding works. It's where all the volatile oils of the lemon are hidden, and what gives this dessert its intensity of flavor. I first tasted it at Antica Dolceria Bonajuto, where some of Sicily's most ancient recipes have been preserved and are still prepared.

Zest of 6 lemons—yellow part only removed in thin strips with a vegetable peeler

6 perfect lemons (or six 6-ounce custard cups)

3 cups distilled water

¾ cup sugar

2 tablespoons Lemon Liqueur (limoncello; page 200), optional

5 tablespoons cornstarch

The day before you plan to make the pudding, in a bowl, combine the lemon zest to the water, sugar, and lemon liqueur (if using). Stir to dissolve the sugar. Cover and let infuse overnight. The liquid will turn a brilliant yellow color and become flavored with the oil from the zest. (Reserve the zested lemons for another use. They can be pushed through a fine-mesh strainer to extract the juice.)

If using lemons for serving, slice off the top third of each perfect lemon. Scoop out the pulp and save the pulp for another use as suggested above. Slice a small piece off the bottom of each so they'll stand securely without tipping over. Cover and set aside while you prepare the pudding.

Strain the lemon water into a medium nonreactive saucepan off the heat. Add the cornstarch, a little at a time, whisking constantly until all the cornstarch is dissolved. Set the pan over medium heat and cook, whisking constantly, until the pudding is thickened and clear. Pour into the prepared lemons or custard cups and chill until set before serving, about 3 hours.

MAKES 6 SERVINGS

Very soon after the Arabs landed at Mazara del Vallo in the ninth century, they invented this dessert. Using sugar, jasmine, pistachios, and the juice from the watermelons they brought to Sicily, and the starch from wheat they found already there, they created *gelo di melone.* (The chocolate was a sixteenth-century addition.) During the feast of Santa Rosalia in July, *gelo di melone* is sold from kiosks, carts, and shops all over Palermo.

Watermelon Pudding
Gelo di Melone

One 5-pound ripe, red watermelon

¾ cup sugar

⅔ cup cornstarch

¼ teaspoon cinnamon

1 teaspoon rose water or 2 tablespoons Jasmine Water (acqua di gelsomino; page 63)

⅓ cup semisweet chocolate chips

GARNISH

⅓ cup diced Squash Preserves (zuccata; page 190) or Citron Preserves (conserva di cedro; page 189)

3 tablespoons unsalted pistachios, chopped

Jasmine flowers

Have ready six 6-ounce custard cups, a 6-cup mold, or six small dessert bowls.

Halve or quarter the watermelon, remove the flesh and cut it into chunks, removing and discarding the seeds. Juice the watermelon using a juicing machine, or puree the fruit and press it through a fine-mesh sieve lined with a double thickness of cheesecloth. Discard the pulp, and measure out 4 cups juice.

(continued)

Spoon Sweets

In a large saucepan, whisk together the juice, sugar, cornstarch, and cinnamon until smooth and no lumps of cornstarch remain. Over medium heat, bring the mixture to a boil and cook, whisking constantly, until thickened and glossy, about 7 minutes. Remove from the heat and add the rose water or jasmine water. Let cool until lukewarm, then stir in the chocolate bits.

Spritz the mold(s) with water, then spoon the pudding into them. Refrigerate until well chilled.

Unmold the pudding, or, if using dessert bowls, serve it right in the bowls. Garnish with the squash or citron preserves, pistachios, and jasmine flowers.

MAKES 6 SERVINGS

Benedictine Chocolate Pudding
Gelo di Cioccolato

The Benedictine Monastery of San Nicola in Catania was founded in the early eighteenth century as a repository for the second-born sons of nobility, who could inherit titles but not land and wealth. Nonetheless, the monastery received generous endowments by the families so their sons might continue to live a comfortable, though frugal, existence. They apparently suffered few ills. In a journal recovered in 1988 from the monastery, strict sumptuary laws were prescribed by the abbot, stressing *assolutamente* the avoidance of an excess of food, lest the delicate constitutions of the brothers be compromised. The lunch menu for Holy Thursday 1790 is set forth as follows:

FIRST COURSE: fish

SECOND COURSE: soup of bread, anchovies, asparagus, fish, and lentils

THIRD COURSE: more fish—pie of swordfish, bass, asparagus, fennel, and broccoli

FOURTH COURSE: beans with raisins and chestnuts

FIFTH COURSE: *gelo di cioccolato*

. . . followed by apples, dates, raisins, figs, and walnuts. This would tide them over until their light supper of soup, caviar, and dates. The Benedictine recipe for *gelo di cioccolato* calls for water instead of milk, and that is how they make it at Antica Dolceria Bonajuto in Modica, where owner Franco Ruta and his son Pierpaolo dedicate themselves to preserving the history of Sicilian pastry.

2 tablets chocolate from Modica (see Sources)
    or 2 round tablets Ybarra chocolate (see Note), chopped

3 cups milk (or water), divided

¼ cup cornstarch

2 tablespoons chopped unsalted pistachios, optional

2 tablespoons Squash Preserves (zuccata; page 190) optional

Have ready four 6-ounce custard cups or a 1-quart mold.

In a medium saucepan over low heat, melt the chocolate in 2½ cups of the milk (or water), whisking constantly. In a small bowl, combine the remaining ½ cup milk (or water) with the cornstarch, stirring to dissolve the cornstarch, and add to the hot milk mixture. Bring to a boil over medium heat, whisking constantly until thickened. Reduce the heat to low and simmer, whisking for an additional minute, to be sure that the cornstarch is fully cooked. Remove from the heat.

Spritz a thin mist of water onto the inside of the mold(s) and immediately fill the molds (the pudding firms up quickly). Let cool at room temperature for 30 minutes, then chill in the refrigerator for at least 2 hours.

The pudding should slide out of the mold(s) easily when inverted. If not, dip the mold(s) in hot water for 10 seconds and invert again onto individual plates or a platter. Garnish with the pistachios and squash preserves if desired.

MAKES 4 SERVINGS

NOTE: Ybarra is a brand of Mexican chocolate made in the same distinct manner as the chocolate of Modica. It is available at most Latin American groceries.

Milk Pudding

Biancomangiare

Every cuisine has its comfort food, and in Sicily it's *biancomangiare*. No one knows for sure when Sicilian mothers began making this custard to soothe the souls of their loved ones, but it may very well be one of the island's most ancient preparations. Recipes survive from Roman times for a milk custard thickened with eggs, and the Arabs have been making grain-and-nut-thickened puddings for centuries. Sicilians take this dessert even further, often garnishing it with nuts, candied citrus peel, and chocolate.

3 cups milk

½ cup sugar

6 tablespoons cornstarch

1 teaspoon vanilla

1 strip lemon zest

Have ready four 6-ounce custard cups or a 1-quart mold.

In a medium heavy saucepan, off the heat, whisk together the milk, sugar, cornstarch, and vanilla until the cornstarch is fully dissolved and no lumps remain. Add the lemon zest. Bring to a boil over medium heat, whisking constantly until thickened. Turn the heat down and simmer for another minute to be sure that the cornstarch is cooked. Remove from the heat.

Spritz a thin mist of water on the inside of the mold(s). Remove the lemon zest and immediately fill the molds (the pudding firms up quickly). Allow to cool at room temperature for 30 minutes, then refrigerate for at least 2 hours, or until completely cold.

Turn the pudding out of the mold(s) to serve. You may need to dip the mold(s) in hot water for 30 seconds to loosen the pudding.

MAKES 4 SERVINGS

T o experience *biancomangiare di mandorla* in its truest form, you must go to the Caffè Sicilia in Noto. Corrado Assenza and his brother Carlo make a masterful version, using the plump almonds of Avola. Another version, made with delicately toasted almonds, takes on a tawny color and complete clarity of almond flavor. It's difficult to imagine this dish having once been food to convalesce by.

Almond Pudding
Biancomangiare di Mandorla

1 recipe Almond Milk (latte di mandorla; page 204)

½ cup sugar

½ cup cornstarch

Have ready six 6-ounce custard cups or a 1-quart mold.

In a medium heavy saucepan, off the heat, whisk together the almond milk, sugar, and cornstarch until the cornstarch is fully dissolved and no lumps remain. Bring to a boil over medium heat, whisking constantly until thickened. Turn the heat down and simmer for another minute, just to make sure all the cornstarch is fully cooked. Remove from the heat.

Spritz a thin mist of water on the inside of the mold(s). Immediately fill the mold(s) and allow to cool at room temperature for 30 minutes, then refrigerate for at least 2 hours, or until completely cold.

Turn the pudding out of the mold(s) to serve. You may need to dip the mold(s) in hot water for 30 seconds to loosen the pudding.

MAKES 6 SERVINGS

Spoon Sweets

Confections

Torrone

$\mathcal{T}$he most lavish arrays of *torrone*, the general term used to describe the nut-based confections of Sicily, are to be found at street fairs and carnivals. I once spent half a day in a Palermo dental clinic after chipping a tooth on a hunk of rock-hard *torrone* that I couldn't resist buying from a handsome young street vendor. It was blisteringly hot and there he was, shirtless and sweating, hacking off chunks of the stuff with a hammer and chisel. I should have known.

At Caffè del Corso in Taormina, they still sell *coriandoli*, the colored sugar-coated coriander, cumin, and aniseed that are a legacy of the Arabs. For centuries, people used to toss *coriandoli* for good luck at weddings and processions before *confetti*, sugar-coated almonds, became popular. The word *coriandoli* is now used to describe the bits of colored paper that in the United States are called confetti!

Opposite: Torrone

Nut Praline
Croccante

In Sicily, nuts belong to the same family as *frutta secca*, dried fruit. This confection is from I Peccatucci di Mamma Andrea in Palermo, where sultana raisins are thrown into the mix. Golden raisins work just fine in their place. A similar confection, and a specialty of Pasticceria Infurna in Agrigento, is *fastuccata*, dialect for *pistacchiata*, pistachio praline. It makes excellent use of the meaty pistachios that grow in nearby Favara.

1 pound mixed unblanched whole pistachios, almonds, and hazelnuts
   (in any combination)

2 cups sugar

¼ cup water

½ teaspoon cinnamon

½ teaspoon salt

1 cup golden raisins

Preheat the oven to 350 degrees. Have ready an 11 by 17-inch baking sheet.

Spread the nuts on the baking sheet and toast them in the oven for 12 to 15 minutes, or until toasted and fragrant. Rub them, while still warm, in a towel to remove the loose, papery skins. Set aside. Clean and lightly oil the baking sheet.

In a large heavy-bottomed saucepan, with a wooden spoon, stir together the sugar, water, cinnamon, and salt. Stirring constantly, heat over medium heat until the sugar dissolves. Remove the spoon, raise the heat to medium-high, and bring to a boil, swirling the pan *but not stirring*, until the syrup becomes golden brown. Remove from the heat, immediately add the nuts and raisins, and stir until the caramelized sugar completely crystallizes around the nuts and they form clusters.

Scrape the *croccante* out onto the prepared baking sheet and separate it into smaller clusters. Let cool completely, and store airtight.

MAKES ABOUT 1½ POUNDS

P etramennula means "almond stone," and that's only one of its attributes. When chubby, sweet Sicilian almonds together with honey from bees that drink the nectar of orange blossoms and thyme are cooked to a dark, crunchy caramel, then mixed with candied orange peel, Jordan almonds, and cinnamon, you have a brittlelike candy that dates back to the ninth century. Omit the Jordan almonds and orange peel and it's called *torrone alla mandorla*.

1½ cups sugar

½ cup honey

¼ cup water

1 teaspoon cinnamon

1 pound blanched whole almonds, toasted

½ cup colored Jordan almonds

½ cup diced Candied Orange Peel
    (scorzetta d'arancia candita; page 193)

½ lemon

Lightly oil an 11 by 17-inch baking sheet.

In a large heavy-bottomed saucepan, with a wooden spoon, stir together the sugar, honey, water, and cinnamon. Stirring constantly, heat over medium heat until the sugar is dissolved. Turn the heat to medium-high and remove the spoon. Attach a candy thermometer to the pan (it should be immersed in the syrup but not touch the pan's bottom) and bring to a boil *without stirring*. Cook, swirling the pan *but not stirring*, until the mixture darkens and reaches 300 degrees. Add the toasted almonds, Jordan almonds, and orange peel and remove the pan from the heat. Stir the mixture gently to completely coat the almonds with caramel.

Turn the candy out onto the prepared baking sheet and spread it evenly with the cut side of the lemon. Let cool completely, then break into pieces. Store airtight.

MAKES ABOUT 1½ POUNDS

Sesame Brittle
Cubbaita

This sesame confection has remained virtually unchanged since Saracen times, but for the very Sicilian addition of almonds. Go to any Middle Eastern sweet shop or grocery today and you will find its cousin, *qubbayt*. Sesame seeds came to Sicily in the ninth century with the Arabs, and they remain an important ingredient in the island's bread and pastries.

⅓ cup sugar

1 cup honey

2 tablespoons water

½ teaspoon cinnamon

½ cup blanched whole almonds, toasted

1½ cups sesame seeds, toasted

½ lemon

Lightly oil an 11 by 17-inch baking sheet.

In a large heavy-bottomed saucepan, with a wooden spoon, stir together the sugar, honey, water, and cinnamon. Stirring constantly, heat over medium heat until the sugar is dissolved. Turn the heat to medium-high and remove the spoon. Attach a candy thermometer to the pan (it should be immersed in the syrup but not touch the pan's bottom) and bring to a boil *without stirring*. Cook, swirling the pan *but not stirring,* until the syrup begins to darken and reaches 300 degrees. Add the almonds and sesame seeds, remove the pan from the heat, and stir gently to coat the nuts and seeds with the caramel.

Turn the candy out onto the prepared baking sheet and spread it out evenly with the lemon half. Let it cool until set but not hard, and score into 1-inch diamond shapes with a sharp knife. Cool completely and break the diamonds apart. Store airtight.

MAKES ABOUT 1 POUND

The quince is an Asian native that gained popularity in Sicily during the Spanish occupation. It is inedible in its raw state, but it comes to life when cooked, turning a rosy pink and developing a perfumed flavor like that of ripe pears and rose petals. If you are familiar with Latin American cuisine, you will recognize *cotognata* as a cousin of *pasta de membrillo* (quince paste), another gift of the Spaniards.

The molds employed in the making of *cotognata* are of glazed terra-cotta with designs in relief: fish for abundance, the sun as a symbol of Sicily, and various depictions of the Virgin Mary. I bought several vintage molds at the flea market near the cathedral in Palermo. You could just as easily use shallow metal molds, such as tartlet pans, as long as you keep the paste less than 1 inch deep to allow for even drying.

2 pounds quinces (about 5)

Juice of 1 lemon

3½ cups sugar, plus extra for rolling

Bring 4 quarts of water to a boil in a large pot. Meanwhile, halve the quinces and remove the seeds. Add the quinces to the boiling water and boil for 20 to 30 minutes, or until soft. Drain and let cool enough to handle; set the pot aside.

(continued)

Quince Candy
Cotognata

Peel the quinces and press them through a sieve or food mill to obtain a smooth puree. Return to the pot and add the lemon juice and sugar. Cook, stirring, over medium heat until the paste is thick and dense enough to hold its shape.

Scrape the paste into lightly oiled molds or shallow pans to a depth of ½ to ¾ inch.

Dry the paste for 2 to 3 days in the hot sun, in a food dehydrator, or in the oven with the pilot light on. Unmold the candies onto a rack and dry for another few days, or until no longer sticky. If you need to cut the candy into pieces, do so after 2 or 3 days. Roll in sugar and store airtight.

MAKES ABOUT 3 POUNDS

D espite its name, this *mostarda* bears no relation to the "mustard fruit" of the same name from Cremona, in the north of Italy. The name comes from the word *mosto,* or grape must, its principal ingredient.

Made in much the same way as quince candy (*cotognata;* page 181), *mostarda* makes wonderful use of the same terra-cotta molds from Caltagirone. It is kept on hand to serve when the neighbors drop by, along with dried figs, dates, and nuts. The Marciante brothers, who own an elegant pastry shop in Siracusa, parted with the very last piece of *mostarda* from their family stash in the name of research. I had to beg.

5 pounds flavorful red grapes, stems removed

6 egg whites

3 tablespoons sugar

Grated zest of 1 orange

1 teaspoon cinnamon

½ cup cornstarch

¼ cup cold water

½ cup blanched whole almonds, toasted and coarsely chopped

In a food processor or blender, puree the grapes in several batches. Press the puree through a strainer lined with a double thickness of damp cheesecloth to extract the juice. (Better still, put the grapes through a juicer.) Reserve the solids.

Place the juice in a large deep saucepan. Mix 3 cups of the grape solids (discard the rest) with the egg whites and stir into the juice. Place the pan over medium heat and bring to a gentle simmer, without stirring or moving the pan. As the egg whites cook, they will float to the surface, forming what is called a "raft," bringing all the sediment with them and leaving the clarified grape juice underneath.

Confections

✹

Carefully scoop off the raft and ladle out the juice; you need 4 cups. Transfer the clarified juice to a medium saucepan and add the sugar, orange zest, and cinnamon. In a small bowl, dissolve the cornstarch in the cold water, and whisk into the juice. Bring to a boil over medium heat and cook, stirring, until thickened and clear. Stir in the almonds. Remove from the heat.

Spritz 8 to 10 small decorative molds or shallow pans with water. Pour in the grape mixture to a depth of no more than 1 inch. Dry for 2 to 3 days in the hot sun, in a food dehydrator, or in an oven with the pilot light on. If you need to cut the candy into pieces, do so now.

Unmold the *mostarda* and place it on a rack to dry for another few days, until chewy. The longer the *mostarda* dries, the chewier it will get. Store airtight.

MAKES ABOUT 1 POUND

Y ou want to laugh at the vulgarity of it all, but you can't. It's so childlike and sincere. Striped a garish pink, white, and green in lighthearted mimicry of the Italian flag, *gelato di campagna* is a tooth-numbingly sweet takeoff on *pezzi duri*, molded ice creams, which they are meant to resemble. It's interesting to note that when I'm working as a food stylist, this is almost the exact mixture I use to create fake ice cream that won't melt under the hot lights.

Fondant Candy
Gelato di Campagna

Three 7½-ounce jars marshmallow cream

2 pounds powdered sugar

½ teaspoon almond extract

Cornstarch for dusting

½ cup blanched whole almonds, toasted

Red and green food coloring

Line an 8 by 4-inch loaf pan with baking parchment or plastic wrap.

In a lightly oiled large mixing bowl, combine the marshmallow cream, powdered sugar, and almond extract, stirring with a wooden spoon until the mixture comes together in a ball. Dust your hands and a work surface lightly with cornstarch. Transfer the mixture to the work surface and knead until very smooth. Knead in the almonds.

Divide the mixture into 3 pieces and color 1 piece with green food coloring (be bold!) and 1 piece with pink (bold again), leaving the third piece white. Press the *gelato* into the prepared loaf pan in 3 even layers, with the white in the middle, cover with plastic wrap, and refrigerate for at least 2 hours.

When ready to serve, turn the candy out of the loaf pan, remove the plastic wrap, and cut into 1-inch-thick slices with a sharp, sharp knife.

MAKES 8 SLICES

Confections

Preserves

Conserve

$\mathcal{M}$y mother has a jar of orange marmalade that is thirty-three years old—the last jar of the last batch made by her grandmother. It's much more than a jar of oranges and sugar. It has heart.

The Romans were preserving fruits in honey in the first century. Apicius gives instructions for how to keep grapes, quinces, figs, apples, plums, pears, cherries, citron, mulberries, and pomegranates in his book *Cookery and Dining in Imperial Rome:* put them in a jar of honey. The recipe for stuffed figs in this chapter was given to me by a woman in Linguaglossa. It is almost identical to Apicius' two-thousand-year-old recipe. Little has changed since the ninth century, when the Arabs brought citrus fruits and sugarcane to Sicily and taught the Sicilians how to preserve the peel and make marmalades.

There are two producers of Sicilian preserves who stand head and shoulders above the others: I Peccatucci di Mamma Andrea in Palermo and Caffè Sicilia in Noto. "Mamma" Andrea di Cesare (the *peccatucci* are her "little sins") began crafting her preserves—more than thirty kinds—in a tiny shop on the Via Principe di Scordia. They are now sold all over Italy and as far away as Japan. At Caffè Sicilia, the Assenza brothers' recipes are a closely guarded secret (as they should be), but they will ship their product to the United States (see Sources).

Pistachio Preserves
Conserva di Pistacchi

This is too simple not to try at least once. *Conserva di pistacchi* is essential in the making of a *trionfo di gola* ("triumph of gluttony," page 142) and can be used instead of jam or jelly as a filling for cookies and pastries.

1 pound shelled raw pistachios

2 cups sugar

½ cup water

In a medium bowl, pour boiling water over the pistachios and allow to sit for 3 minutes. Drain the pistachios and rub them in a cloth towel to remove the papery skins. In a food processor or coffee grinder, grind the nuts to a powder.

In a heavy saucepan, bring the sugar and water to a boil over medium heat, stirring constantly. When the sugar is dissolved, add the ground pistachios and continue to cook, stirring constantly, until thick. Store tightly covered in the refrigerator for up to 3 months.

MAKES ABOUT 2 PINTS

T he *cedro,* or citron, is what I call a biblical fruit. That is to say, it has remained untouched by hybridizing hands since pre-Christian times.

Citron Preserves
Conserva di Cedro

Known as the *etrog* in Hebrew, it is put to ritual use at Sukkot, the Jewish Festival of the Tabernacles, during the harvest season. The citron resembles a huge, lumpy lemon, and between the rather thin skin and the small pocket of pulp there is a vast area of soft white pith that is used to make this preserve. Milder than the pith of a lemon, it makes a delicious snack on its own, thinly sliced and sprinkled with sugar or salt. The tartness of citron as a preserve is a great counterpoint to the sweetness of certain pastries.

3 fresh citrons (approximately 1 pound each!), available in
  gourmet markets or Middle Eastern groceries

One 3-inch cinnamon stick, broken

4 cups sugar

1 cup water

Wash the citrons in cold water and cut into quarters. Remove the seeds. Grate the citrons, including the peel and white membrane, on the largest holes of a box grater.

Place the grated citron in a bowl with the cinnamon stick and cover with cold water. Let sit for 24 hours, draining and adding fresh cold water every 6 hours. Drain and squeeze the fruit to extract as much liquid as possible. In a large heavy saucepan, stir together the sugar and water. Add the citron and cinnamon, bring to a boil over medium heat, and cook, stirring, until most of the syrup has been absorbed and the fruit is translucent.

Remove the cinnamon stick and pack the preserves into sterilized jars, filling them to ¼ inch from the top. Wipe off the rims, screw on the lids, and turn the jars upside down; leave them undisturbed for 12 hours. They should be vacuum-sealed, but if not, just refrigerate them for up to 3 months.

MAKES ABOUT 6 PINTS

Squash Preserves
Zuccata

I f you've ever had pickled watermelon rind, this will seem vaguely familiar. *Zuccata*, also known as *cucuzzata*, after the mother squash, *cucuzza*, shows up again and again in Sicilian pastry. The squash in its raw state is tough and insipid, lacking much character of its own. To call someone a *cucuzz'* is to say he or she possesses such qualities. Characterizations aside, the poor *cucuzza* is unavailable in the United States. An underripe melon or an old, has-been zucchini is an acceptable substitute. The sugar and floral water, combined with soaking and cooking, go a long way toward transforming its flavor, which becomes delicate and perfumed.

2 pounds large, past-its-prime zucchini
or one 2-pound underripe honeydew melon

1 tablespoon salt

3 cups sugar

1 cup Jasmine Water (acqua di gelsomino;
page 63) or 2 tablespoons rose water

1 cup water

Peel the zucchini or melon, halve, remove the seeds, and cut into ½-inch cubes. Sprinkle with the salt, place in a colander, and leave for 1 hour to drain.

Rinse the salt off the squash or melon and squeeze gently to extract the excess salty liquid. Soak in water to cover for 12 hours, changing the water 3 or 4 times.

Drain the fruit and squeeze gently again to extract the excess liquid. Transfer to a large saucepan and add the sugar, jasmine or rose water, and water. Simmer, stirring, for 40 to 50 minutes, or until the syrup is thickened and the fruit is translucent. Store tightly covered in the refrigerator for up to 3 months.

MAKES ABOUT 3 PINTS

Bar Saint Honoré

TAORMINA

Connie di Bella of the Bar Saint Honoré is the unofficial queen of Sicily's famous resort town, Taormina, which clings to a cliff on the east coast. The allure of Bar Saint Honoré is not the pastry, although it is fine, but the bar itself—and Madame Connie. There she sits, perched on a bar stool at her cash register, dripping in expensive costume jewelry, pecking out the sales with manicured nails of a pistachio-shell red.

Even though this is a town where the European swells and dandies strut their stuff, you wonder what a glamour-puss like Connie is doing here. She doesn't even bake—"I don't want to learn; then the people will want me to do it"—and is so fancy she seems better suited to the *dolce vita* lifestyle of the people she serves. But Taormina is her empire and the bar her

castle. "Oh, *darrrling*," she purrs, "you must try some of my almond wine!"

Connie was born in Caccamo, a small town near Palermo (of course she won't say when), and left at the age of fourteen to marry an American. They settled in Astoria, New York, where she gave birth to two boys, and then her husband died.

Connie is proud of her time in the United States. After the death of her husband, she moved the family to Los Angeles, where she worked as a waitress, spinning salads and serving up T-bones to the likes of Carlo Gambino. Sometime in the sixties she met her second husband, a Sicilian who operated a swanky nightclub on the Sunset Strip. Together they owned restaurants in Los Angeles and San Francisco before moving back to Sicily in the early nineties.

Setting up shop in Taormina, they owned a restaurant, then Bar Saint Honoré. And then her second husband died. Connie wore black and mourned dutifully for about three days, then quickly got back to business. There is always a crowd of men around her, but Connie seems unfazed. "What use do I have for another husband? I have my family, my friends, and my shop. *E basta!*"

Come here once, and you're family. Everyone who works for her is the same way. Antonio knows just how you like your *caffè,* and his wife, Mariella, will bring you those same little cookies you liked so much yesterday. Signora Maria worries that the sandwich you just ate has not filled you up. So Ignazio brings a plateful of the buttery *biscottini di tè* with your *cappuccino.* Free. It's that kind of place.

Looking for a bedspread? Connie has a friend with a shop. Need to change some money during off-hours? She'll make a call. Looking for a husband? She can hook you up. One evening, we got cocky and left the car parked in the *piazza.* It was towed. Connie phoned her friend the *vigile urbano,* traffic officer, who abandoned his own supper to hop a moped and come to our rescue. People *do* things for Connie.

To be fair, I should mention the pastries. The *vetrina,* or window display, is one of the most beautiful in town, and as fancy as the Queen herself. Pyramids of glittering, jewellike candied fruits nuzzle up alongside buttery tea cookies (*biscottini di tè*) and hazelnut meringues (*croccantini*)—specialties of her chef, Orazio. And in Taormina, there is no better way to start your day than with Orazio's buttery, sweet breakfast pastries, still warm from the oven.

And a hug from Connie.

Candied Orange Peel
Scorzetta d'Arancia Candita

At Bar Saint Honoré in Taormina, you can buy whole candied oranges, as well as beautiful wedges of candied peel. The bitter little squares of gummy fruit that pass as candied orange peel in the United States are no match at all for the homemade variety. No wonder most people hate them. The profusion of oranges in Sicily ensures an abundant supply of fruit for this confection. Since you can hardly be expected to make real Sicilian pastry without it, get hold of some California or Florida navel oranges and make your own. Then you'll see what all the fuss is about.

3 unblemished organic navel oranges

2 cups sugar

⅓ cup water

¼ cup corn syrup

Wash the oranges and cut each one into 6 wedges. Scrape away the pulp (reserve it for another use), leaving the peel with the white membrane attached, and place the peel into a nonreactive saucepan.

Cover the orange peel with cold water and bring to a boil. Boil for 1 minute, then drain off the water. Cover again with cold water, bring to a boil, and drain; repeat the process 2 more times. This is the only way to remove the bitterness from the peel; you'll be glad you went to the trouble.

Remove the peel from the saucepan and add the sugar, water, and corn syrup to the pan. Bring to a boil over medium-high heat, stirring constantly to dissolve the sugar. When the sugar is dissolved, add the peel, turn the heat down to medium, and boil for 20 to 25 minutes, or until most of the syrup is absorbed and the peel is glossy.

Place a cooling rack over a baking sheet to catch drips, and transfer the wedges of candied peel to the rack. Let cool and dry for 2 to 3 hours, then store airtight in the refrigerator for up to 6 months.

MAKES ABOUT 1 POUND

Blood Orange Marmalade
Marmellata di Tarocchi

Forgo the mammoth *autostrada* and take the minor road from Acireale toward Taormina, where lush groves of citrus fruits blanket the countryside. From December to May, the *tarocco,* or blood orange, is a must-try. Look for the dark ruby-fleshed *moro* variety, especially prized for its sweetness and perfume.

This recipe was given to me by a Frenchwoman living in Sicily named Jacqueline, who had better things to do than spend the traditional three days making marmalade. *C'est deliziosa!*

Equal weights of blood oranges, sugar, and water

Costumi Siciliani · Raccolto delle arance

Wash the oranges and remove the stems. Slice crosswise ⅛ inch thick, working over a bowl to catch the juices. Pick out all the seeds and discard. Weigh the oranges with their juice and place them in a bowl. Weigh out an equal amount of water and add to the oranges in the bowl. Weigh out the same amount of sugar and set aside until later. Cover the bowl and leave at room temperature for 12 to 18 hours.

Transfer the contents of the bowl to a large non-copper, nonaluminum saucepan. Stir in the sugar and place the pan over medium heat. Bring to a boil, stirring constantly to dissolve the sugar. Turn the heat down to a simmer and continue to cook for about 2 hours, stirring occasionally. After the first hour of cooking, the marmalade will begin to thicken. At this point, stir frequently until the marmalade thickens enough to pull away from the sides of the pan. Test the marmalade by dropping a teaspoonful on a cold plate. It should set up and not run when it cools.

When the marmalade is ready, ladle it into sterilized jars to ¼ inch from the top. Wipe off the rims, screw on the lids, and turn the jars upside down. Allow to cool for 12 hours undisturbed, then turn upright. The lids should be vacuum-sealed; if not, store the marmalade in the refrigerator for up to 6 months.

Sweet Sicily

EACH POUND OF ORANGES YIELDS APPROXIMATELY 4 PINTS

The slopes of Mount Etna, Sicily's active volcano, are covered six months out of the year in snow, making it a popular—if dicey—destination for skiers. The favorite resort is in a town called Linguaglossa, on Etna's north flank. Linguaglossa's rich volcanic soil nourishes the plump, luscious figs that appear once the snow melts.

Nut-Filled Figs in Wine
Fichi Ripieni sotto Vino

12 large just-ripe fresh figs

½ cup blanched whole almonds, toasted

½ cup walnut halves, toasted

1 teaspoon unsweetened cocoa

1 teaspoon vanilla

2 to 3 tablespoons honey

6 whole cloves

3 bay leaves

Two 3-inch cinnamon sticks

3 cups Cooked Grape Must Syrup (vino cotto; page 202) or honey

Preheat the oven to 325 degrees. Lightly oil a baking sheet.

Split the figs lengthwise just three-quarters of the way through, leaving the stem end intact. Scoop out about a half-teaspoonful of fruit from each half.

In a food processor or in an electric coffee grinder, in small batches, grind the nuts with the cocoa, vanilla, and just enough honey to make a stiff paste. Fill each fig with a tablespoonful of this mixture and press the halves together, enclosing the filling as much as possible.

Transfer the figs to the oiled baking sheet and bake for 25 to 30 minutes, or until they are rather dry and beginning to brown. Let cool completely and layer in a glass jar with the cloves and bay leaves. Tuck in the cinnamon sticks and pour in enough *vino cotto* or honey to cover. Store in the refrigerator, but bring to room temperature before serving.

MAKES ABOUT 1½ QUARTS

Liqueurs and Beverages

Liquori e Bevandi

Libiamo, libiamo ne' calici che la bellezza infiora...
Let's drink from the mirth-giving cup that beauty adorns...

La Traviata, Giuseppe Verdi

As far back as the earliest Greek colonists, Sicilians have been concocting beverages whose importance goes far beyond that of mere refreshment. The earliest wine may have been the honey wine of the Greeks, used at wedding ceremonies then as now. The Romans made a sweet wine of rose petals that was used as a laxative. The Arabs, whose religion forbade the drinking of alcohol, used the anise-flavored *zammù* as a disinfectant. *Vino cotto* and *mosto cotto* are syrups made from the boiled-down must of grapes; both have been around in their present form since Roman times.

Almost every bar in Sicily has at least one bottle of homemade something. *Limoncello,* made with the fragrant Sicilian lemons, and *mandarinetto* are two of the most common. And each region in Sicily has a sweet wine for which it is famous: Malvasia in Lipari and Messina, Zibibbo in Pantelleria, Moscato in Siracusa, and Marsala in—where else—Marsala. And you can't go anywhere near Catania without running into *vino alla mandorla,* almond wine.

The ancient Greeks believed that almonds possessed mystical, even magical, powers. Anyone who has seen the portrait of Priapus, god of strength and virility, at Pompeii can attest to the veracity of this claim. Their blossoming signaled the period of fertility, for man as well as beast, and Priapus liked to eat some with his wine. The idea of mixing the two came to an alchemist in a night vision involving Dionysius, god of wine, and Priapus, and *vino alla mandorla* was born.

The *vino alla mandorla* at the Bar Turrisi in Castelmola is made from Gaglioppo grapes and Catanian almonds, both bitter and sweet, and is ready to drink after a six-month fermentation. It's best served ice-cold with a squeeze of orange and a couple of *quaresimali* (Lenten biscuits).

Honey Wine
Idromele

Here is the recipe for a honey wine similar to the one served at Greek and Roman wedding ceremonies. It is almost identical, in fact, to a recipe for *hydromeli* that appears in Apicius' *Cookery and Dining in Imperial Rome,* written two thousand years ago. That one called for newly fallen rainwater!

4 cups distilled water

2 cups honey

1 cup vodka or brandy

Bring the water and honey to a boil in a medium saucepan. Boil until reduced by half. Let cool, then stir in the vodka or brandy.

Pour into a glass jar, cover, and store in a cool dark place for 1 month before drinking.

MAKES 1 QUART

Tangerine Liqueur
Mandarinetto

Tangerines came to Sicily with the Arabs in the ninth century. The same citrus groves they planted over a thousand years ago still flourish in the Conca d'Oro, or Fertile Crescent, just outside of Palermo. Like a heady little sip of sunshine, *mandarinetto* is more than a mere beverage. It's an indispensable and purely Sicilian flavoring for many pastries, used in much the same way as vanilla. One day in Taormina, my bartender friend Antonio rushed past me on the road carrying an armload of freshly picked tangerines. By the time I caught up with him at Bar Saint Honoré, he had already begun turning the fruit into a batch of golden *mandarinetto*. Here is his recipe.

10 organic tangerines, washed

1 quart vodka

3 cups sugar

4 cups water

With a vegetable peeler, remove all the zest (orange part only) from the tangerines and place in a glass jar with a tight-fitting lid. Add the vodka and leave in a cool dark place for 1 month.

After the month has passed, combine the sugar and water in a saucepan and bring to a boil, stirring until the sugar is dissolved. Let cool completely.

Add the sugar syrup to the vodka mixture. Strain to remove the zest and pour into glass bottles. This keeps indefinitely if stored in a cool place. Serve chilled.

MAKES 2 QUARTS

Antonio's Lemon Liqueur

Limoncello all'Antonio

Show up at the Bar Saint Honoré in Taormina any day except Tuesday after 3 P.M., and Antonio Sapia will be there tending bar. He will give you a dish of olives that he cured himself and engage you in a discussion of sex, friendship, and money, using the lemons from his garden to demonstrate. While his philosophy is nothing you haven't already heard, the *limoncello* he makes with those greenish-yellow lemons is like nothing you've ever tasted. If you have access to Meyer lemons, use them. Their flavor is closer to the spiciness of the Sicilian variety.

10 organic lemons, washed

1 quart vodka

2 cups sugar

3 cups water

With a vegetable peeler, remove all the zest (yellow part only) from the lemons and place it in a glass jar with a tight-fitting lid. Add the vodka and leave in a cool dark place for 1 month.

After the month has passed, combine the sugar and water in a saucepan and bring to a boil, stirring until the sugar is dissolved. Let cool completely.

Add the sugar syrup to the vodka mixture. Strain to remove the lemon zest and pour into glass bottles. This keeps indefinitely if stored in a cool place. Serve chilled.

MAKES 2 QUARTS

Anise Liqueur
Zammù

Zammù began life as an anti-fungal, introduced to Sicily by the Arabs. Then someone discovered that you could drink it. Now it's enjoyed for its own sake, delicious alone or topping off an espresso, turning the espresso into a *caffè corretto*. *Zammù* tastes a lot like *sambuca*, *ouzo*, or Pernod, all anise-based liquors.

1 quart vodka

¾ cup aniseed

One 3-inch cinnamon stick, broken

2 tablespoons coriander seed

2 whole cloves

1 strip orange zest

2½ cups sugar

2 cups water

In a glass jar with a tight-fitting lid, combine the vodka, spices, and orange zest. Leave in a cool dark place for 2 months.

After the 2 months have passed, combine the sugar and water in a saucepan and bring to a boil, stirring until the sugar is dissolved. Let cool completely.

Add the sugar syrup to the vodka mixture. Filter through a double thickness of damp cheesecloth set in a strainer and pour into a glass bottle. *Zammù* keeps indefinitely if stored in a cool dark place, and it will improve in flavor.

MAKES ABOUT 1½ QUARTS

Cooked Grape Must Syrup

VINO COTTO

This is one of Sicily's most ancient sweeteners, made from the boiled-down must (juice) of freshly pressed red grapes. Arriving in Sicily during the *vendemmia,* or grape harvest, doesn't automatically assure you an ample supply of *vino cotto.* You have to know where to find it. *Vino cotto* is not sold in stores—in fact, as far as I can tell, it's not sold at all. I know—I tried desperately to find some. People, I was told, have it in their homes. So I asked everyone I met if they had any in their home. After almost three weeks, I hit a vein.

I had invited myself to a San Martino party held at a chicken farm in the hills above Taormina and was sharing a table with a very spry older couple who lived in the town. While the husband tangoed with all the girls, I asked his wife, Giuseppina, The Question.

"Why don't you just make some yourself?" asked Giuseppina. "It's *molto facile,*" very easy.

Twenty minutes later, after relating to me her *"molto facile"* recipe, Giuseppina finally admitted she had one bottle left at home.

"Meet me tomorrow morning at ten o'clock sharp at this address, which is just behind the Bank of Sicily. Go around to the back and up to the second floor and push the button marked 3C. I will meet you there with the *vino cotto.* Don't be late."

I am still mourning that bottle of *vino cotto,* which exploded in my suitcase on the plane. I am not ashamed to say I licked some off my cosmetic case, and it was delicious.

Here, in her own words, is Giuseppina's recipe:

"*Ah, signorina, è molto facile!* First you procure the must."

"How much must?" I asked.

"As much as the grapes give you."

"Then?"

"Then you burn some of the dried vine cuttings and save the ashes."

"How many vines?"

"Not too many. Then put the ashes and the must in a pot. Not aluminum. Then you boil it."

"For how long?"

"Not too long."

"And do you stir it?"

"Yes. With the branch of a tangerine tree. Or even wild fennel. *Molto facile.* Then you let it rest for twenty-four hours. Afterward, spoon out the good part and leave the bad."

"The good part being the liquid?"

"Of course. Unless you like the taste of ashes. Speaking of taste, some people put in orange peel, or cinnamon, or even cloves, but I don't. Mine are very good grapes."

"How much of these spices do you think those people put?"

"Oh, not too much. So, returning to the subject, you boil it until four parts cook down to one part. Then you bottle it *ermetica-mente.*"

"Like for marmalade?"

"No, no, *signorina.* The usual way. *Molto facile.*"

You may want to try this method:

Wash 5 pounds of flavorful red grapes (Muscat are best), and remove the stems. In a food processor or blender, puree the grapes in several batches. Press the puree through a strainer lined with a double thickness of damp cheesecloth to extract the juice. Or, put the grapes through a juicing machine. In either case, save the solids. Pour the juice into a nonreactive saucepan.

In a bowl, mix 6 egg whites with the skins and seeds left from juicing. Add this mixture to the juice. Simmer very slowly over low heat, without stirring, until the egg whites are cooked and rise to the surface, bringing the impurities with them. Carefully spoon off the solids and pour the clear juice through a fine-mesh strainer lined with a double thickness of dampened cheesecloth to remove any stray bits.

Return the clarified juice to the saucepan, and if you wish, add a small strip of orange zest, 3 whole cloves, and a small cinnamon stick. Boil the juice over medium heat until reduced by three-quarters and syrupy. Remove the orange zest and spices, if you used them, and let cool completely. Store in a tightly closed bottle or jar in the refrigerator for up to 6 months.

MAKES ABOUT 1 CUP

Almond Milk

Latte di Mandorla

Sicily's first colonizers were the Greeks, who arrived there twenty-five hundred years ago to find rolling hills covered in blossoming almond trees. This is one of the first beverages the settlers prepared with their newfound bounty. Today, *latte di mandorla* is at the heart of many Sicilian sweets, among them milk pudding (*biancomangiare*), almond syrup (*orzata*), and almond milk sherbet (*cremolata*). At the Antica Dolceria Bonajuto in Modica, and at pastry shops throughout the island, you can purchase 200-gram cakes of a special almond paste that, diluted in water, make a delicious almond milk.

> *2 cups blanched whole almonds*
>
> *4 peach or apricot kernels (see Almonds, page 43) or ¼ teaspoon pure almond extract*
>
> *6 cups cold distilled water*

Soak the almonds and peach or apricot kernels (if using) in the water for 2 to 3 hours.

In a blender or food processor, puree in small batches (with the extract, if using) until smooth. Line a strainer with a double thickness of damp cheesecloth and place it over a large bowl. Pour the almond puree through the strainer, pressing with the back of a spoon to extract as much liquid as possible. Store tightly covered in the refrigerator for up to 3 days.

MAKES ABOUT 1 QUART

T he Spanish were very busy in the fifteenth and sixteenth centuries. Occupying both Sicily and Mexico, they sailed back and forth, cross-pollinating the cuisines of both places. Sicily was to reap the greater benefits, receiving gifts of chocolate, tomatoes, cactus, and peppers. This beverage is one of the few things that made the journey from east to west.

Over the centuries, Mexican cooks have swapped almonds for the original rice, and orange flower water for cinnamon, and there the drink is now known as *horchata*. In Spain, present-day Catalonians prepare several versions of *orxata* (the Catalonian spelling), using almonds, sprouting barley, and even *chufa*, or tiger nuts, which aren't nuts at all, but rather nut-shaped growths that cling to the roots of a tuber. *Orzata* is used to make almond milk sherbet (*cremolata di mandorla*) and as a base for a cooling summer drink. Fill a glass with ice and pour in half *orzata* and half sparkling water.

Almond Syrup
Orzata

> 4 cups Almond Milk (*latte di mandorla*; page 204)
>
> 1 tablespoon orange flower water (see Sources)
>
> 3 cups sugar

Combine all the ingredients in a large saucepan. Bring to a boil over medium-high heat, stirring constantly to dissolve the sugar, and continue to boil for 5 to 8 minutes, or until the sugar is completely dissolved and the *orzata* is slightly thickened. Let cool completely.

Bottle and store in the refrigerator for up to 2 weeks.

MAKES ABOUT 1½ QUARTS

Pomegranate Syrup
Sciroppo di Melagrano

Pomegranates have long been important in Sicily, where they are remembered in flesh and in myth. Persephone, daughter of Demeter, the goddess of grain, was said to have been abducted from Sicily by Pluto, god of the underworld. In her grief, Demeter caused darkness and cold to envelop the world for as long as her daughter remained in hell. A deal was struck whereby Pluto would return Persephone to her mother for part of each year. Her yearly descent back into the underworld (which corresponds almost exactly with the winter solstice) marks the beginning of winter. Persephone is always depicted holding a pomegranate, the symbol of rebirth.

Diluted with sparkling water and served over ice, this syrup makes a refreshing summer drink.

8 large pomegranates or 2 cups pomegranate juice (available in
health food stores and Middle Eastern markets)

2 cups sugar

3 cups water

If using pomegranates, cut them into quarters and pull out the seeds. Put the seeds through a juicing machine or press them through a fine-mesh strainer to remove the juice. Measure out 2 cups juice and drink the rest.

In a large saucepan, bring the sugar and water to a boil, stirring constantly until the sugar is dissolved. Boil for 5 minutes. Add the pomegranate juice and boil for another 10 minutes. Let cool.

Pour the syrup into bottles and refrigerate for up to 6 months.

MAKES ABOUT 1 QUART

Sicilian Pastry Shops

ACIREALE

Pasticceria G. Castorina
Corso Umberto I 63

Gelateria Costarelli
Piazza Duomo

Pasticceria Papillon
Corso Umberto I 130

AGRIGENTO

Pasticceria la Promenade
Via Panoramica dei Templi 8

Bar Sajeva
Viale della Vittoria 61/65

Bar Pasticceria la Galleria
Via Atenea 123

Badia Santo Spirito
Via Santo Spirito

Pasticceria Infurna
Via Atenea

ALCAMO

Pasticceria San Gaetano
Via San Gaetano 16

AUGUSTA

Bar Pasticceria Nuovo Alberobello
Via Umberto I 146

Pasticceria lo Giudice
Via Umberto I 286

Eurobar
Via Principe Umberto I 256

BAGHERIA

Gelateria Anni '20
Via Mattarella 13

BRONTE

Conti Gallenti
Corso Umberto I 275

CALTANISSETTA

Bar Pasticceria Fiorino
Via E. Vassallo 67

Pasticceria Cordaro e Toscano
Via dei Mille 42

Caffè Pasticceria Rair
Corso Umberto 163

CANICATTÌ

Pasticceria Carusotto
Via Garilli 17

Pasticceria Mantione
Via Cavour 154

CASTELMOLA

Bar Turrisi
Piazza del Duomo

Caffè San Giorgio
Piazza Sant'Antonio 1

CATANIA

Pasticceria Savia
Via Etnea 302

Caprice
Via Etnea 30

Pasticceria Mantegna
Via Etnea 350

Privitera
Piazza Santa Maria del Gesù 1–2

Nuovo Caffè Italia
Corso Italia 247

St. Moritz
Viale R. Sanzio 4–12

CORLEONE

Bentivegna
Piazza Vittorio Emanuele 1

ENNA

Pasticceria il Dolce
Piazza Sant'Agostino 40

Bar Pasticceria Caprice
Via Firenze 17

Pasticceria Rugolo
Via Roma 425

ERICE

Pasticceria Maria
Via Vittorio Emanuele 14

FAVARA

Antico Caffè Italia
Piazza Cavour 1

GELA

Bar Pasticceria Buongiorno
Corso Vittorio Emanuele 338

Bar Pasticceria Incardona
Via Navarra 98

GIARDINI NAXOS

Caffè Cavallaro
Via Umberto 165

Bar Pasticceria Salamone
Via Vittorio Emanuele 236

LAMPEDUSA

Bar Roma
Via E. Duse 1

LENTINI

Pasticceria Navarria
Via Conte Alaimo 12

LETOJANNI

Pasticceria Caminiti
Via Vittorio Emanuele 227

LICATA

Pasticceria Porrello
Via Stazione Vecchia 14

LIPARI

Bar Pasticceria Subba
Via Vittorio Emanuele 92

Bar Oscar
Via Vittorio Emanuele 74

Pasticceria del Corso
Corso Vittorio Emanuele 232

MARSALA

Pasticceria Lilibeo
Via Salemi 5

Pasticceria Tahiti
Contrada Casazze 22

MELILLI

Pasticceria Scamporrino
Via Dante Alighieri 7

MESSINA

Pasticceria Irrera
Piazza Cairoli 7

Pasticceria Vinci Domenico
Via Garibaldi 429

Bar Pasticceria Pisani
Via Tommaso Cannizzaro 45

Pasticceria Bille
Piazza Cairoli 9

Pasticceria la Spada
Via Natoli 19

MISTRETTA

Italia di Capicotto Anna
Corso Umberto I 2

Pasticceria Testa
Via Monte 2

Primavera
Via Primavera 14

MODICA

Antica Dolceria Bonajuto
Corso Umberto I 159

MONREALE

Bar Pasticceria Mirto
Piazza Guglielmo 13

NOTO

Caffè Sicilia
Corso Vittorio Emanuele 125

Pasticceria Corrado Costanzo
Via Silvio Spaventa 7/9

PALAZZOLO ACREIDE

Antica Pasticceria Corsino
Via Nazionale 2

PALERMO

Spinnato il Golosone
Piazza Castelnuovo 16

Bar Pasticceria Mazzara
Via Generale Magliocco 15

I Peccatucci di Mamma Andrea
Via Principe di Scordia 67

Caflisch la Capannina
Viale Regina Margherita 2/B
Mondello

Antico Chiosco
Piazza Mondello 4
Mondello

Fratelli Magri
Via Isidoro Carini 42

Pasticceria di Stefano
Via Aquileia 116

Gelateria Liberty
Via Principe di Belmonte 100/A

Pasticceria Costa
Via d'Annunzio 15

Bar Pasticceria Alba
Piazza San Giovanni Bosco 7/C

Pasticceria Svizzera e Siciliana
Via Mariano Stabile 155

Bar Stancapiano
Via Notarbartolo 51

PATERNÒ

Gran Caffè Italia
Piazza Regina Margherita 12

PATTI

Bar Pasticceria Jolie
Via Trieste 20

Pasticceria del Bignè
Via XX Settembre

Pasticceria Pratico
Via Vittorio Emanuele 10

PIANA DEGLI ALBANESI

Pasticceria di Noto
Via Portella della Ginestra 79/81

Pasticceria Elena
Via G. Matteotti 36

PRIZZI

Pasticceria Compagno
Corso Finocchiaro Aprile 30

RAGUSA

Pasticceria di Pasquale
Corso Vittorio Veneto 104

Caffè Pasticceria Ambassador
Via Archimede 6

RANDAZZO

Musumeci
Piazza Santa Maria 5

SAN CATALDO

Pasticceria Gelateria Sollami
Via Garibaldi 93

SCIACCA

Bar Gelateria la Favola
Corso Vittorio Emanuele 234

Pasticceria Pierrot
Via Licata 6

SIRACUSA

Bar Pasticceria Marciante
Via Saverio Landolina 7/9

Gelateria Bianca
Corso Umberto

Pasticceria Rizzo
Viale Polibio 78

Bar Pasticceria Tunisi
Viale Tunisi 74

Bar Nuovo Centrale
Piazza Archimede 22

Bar Duomo
Piazza Duomo 16

TAORMINA

Pasticceria Etna
Corso Umberto 112

Pasticceria Roberto
Via Calapitrulli 9

Bar Saint Honoré
Corso Umberto 208

Caffè del Corso
Corso Umberto 150

TERMINI IMERESE

Pasticceria del Vicolo
Via Mazzarino 100

Pasticceria Cristal
Via Vittorio Amedeo 58

TRAPANI

Bar Pasticceria Colicchia
Via delle Arti 6/8

Pasticceria '900
Via G. B. Fardella 84

Caffè Classique
Via G. B. Fardella 112

Sources

BRUNO BAKERY
506 LaGuardia Place
New York, NY 10012
212-982-5854
602 Lorimer Street
Brooklyn, NY 11211
718-349-6524
Frutta martorana *from Sicily,* cannoli *shells; this Sicilian bakery is a good place to sample pastries as they are made in Sicily.*

BUONITALIA
75 Ninth Avenue
New York, NY 10011
212-633-9090
Frutta martorana *from Sicily, 00 flour, almonds, Sicilian sea salt, candied orange and citron peel, rose water, Jordan almonds, almond milk, orange flower water, almond syrup,* cotognata *from Sicily.*

CAFFÈ SICILIA
Corso Vittorio Emanuele 125
Noto, Italy
0931.83.5013
Fax 0931.83.9781
Best-quality handmade Sicilian marmalades, pistachio and other preserves, torrone *from Sicily.*

COACH FARM DAIRY
Pine Plains, NY 12567
518-398-5325
Goat's milk ricotta—call for retail outlets.

KALUSTYAN'S
123 Lexington Avenue
New York, NY 10016
212-685-3451
Fax: 212-683-8458
www.kalustyans.com
A Middle Eastern market with extensive selection of nuts, spices, sesame seeds, and dried fruits; also sells pomegranate juice and honey.

MOZZARELLA COMPANY
2944 Elm Street
Dallas, TX 75226
800-798-2954
Fax 214-741-4076
MozzCo@aol.com
Goat's milk ricotta by mail order.

NEW YORK CAKE AND BAKING CENTER
56 West 22nd Street
New York, NY 10010
212-675-2253
Nycake@aol.com
Ready-made marzipan in bulk, food coloring, gum arabic, casting gel for making martorana *molds, seashell molds, Jordan almonds, vanilla powder and extract, Ghirardelli chocolate,* cannoli *tubes; mail-order catalog available for $3.00.*

TODARO BROTHERS
555 Second Avenue
New York, NY 10016
212-679-7766
www.todarobros.com

Nuts, sesame seeds in bulk, candied orange and citron peel, 00 flour, spices, imported herb honeys, marmalades, almond milk, almond syrup, orange flower water, Sicilian sea salt; also mail order.

WWW.BUYSICILIAN.IT/UK
Sicilian honey, pastries of Maria Grammatico of Pasticceria Maria in Erice.

WWW.RAGUSAONLINE.COM
Every kind of Sicilian almond product: whole almonds, almond meal, almond flour, almond paste (for making almond milk), almond cookies, martorana, torrone, and "confetti" (sugar-coated almonds); cubbaita *and* mostaccioli del confessore; *and, from the Antica Dolceria Bonajuto, Modican chocolate,* impanatigghe, *and* dolci di riposto.

BRUNO LEOPARDI EDITORE
Via Carducci 3/e
90141 Palermo, Italy
www.brunoleopardi.it
Largest on-line source for books on Sicilian history and culture, many with photographs by Melo Minnella; publisher of the quarterly magazine Sicilia Ritrovata, *dedicated to the preservation of the island's traditions.*

Bibliography

Apicius. *Cookery and Dining in Imperial Rome.* Translated by Joseph Dommers Vehling. New York: Dover Publishing, 1977.

Athenaeus. *The Diepnosophists.* Translated by C. B. Gulick. Cambridge, Mass.: Harvard University Press, 1980.

Atiyeh, Wadeeha. *Scheherazade Cooks.* New York: Gramercy Publishing, 1960.

Buttitta, Antonino, and Melo Minnella. *Sicilia Ritrovata.* Palermo, Sicily: Vito Cavalotto Editrice, 1981.

Buttitta, Antonino. *Le Feste di Pasqua.* Palermo, Sicily: Sicilian Tourist Service, 1990.

Cardella, Antonio. *Sicilia e Isole in Cucina.* Rimini, Italy: Opportunity Books, 1998.

Coria, Giuseppe. *Usi Nuziali e Mangiar di Nozze in Sicilia.* Catania, Sicily: Vito Cavallotto Editrice, 1994.

Correnti, Pino. *Il Libro d'Oro della Cucina e dei Vini di Sicilia.* Milan: Mursia Editrice, 1985.

Costantino, Mario, and Lawrence Gambello. *The Italian Way.* Chicago: Passport Books, 1996.

DiLeo, Maria Adela. *I Dolci Siciliani.* Rome: Newton and Compton, 1998.

Goethe, J. W. *Italian Journey (1786–1788).* Translated by W. H. Auden and Elizabeth Mayer. San Francisco: North Point Press, 1982.

Guercio, Francis. *Sicily: The Garden of the Mediterranean.* London: Faber and Faber, 1968.

Lampedusa, Giuseppe Tomasi di. *The Leopard.* Translated by Archibald Colquhoun. New York: Pantheon Books, 1960.

Malgieri, Nick. *Great Italian Desserts.* Boston: Little, Brown, 1990.

Martial. *Epigrams.* Translated by D. R. Shackleton Bailey. Cambridge, Mass.: Harvard University Press, 1993.

Pavone, Renata Rizzo, and Anna Maria Iozzia. *La Cucina dei Benedettini a Catania.* Catania, Italy: Giuseppe Maimone Editore, 2000.

Pitre, Giuseppe. *La Famiglia, la Casa, la Vita del Popolo Siciliano.* Bologna: Il Vespro, 1969.

Platina, Bartolomeo. *Il Piacere Onesto e la Buona Salute (1475).* Translated by Emilio Faccioli. Turin, Italy: Einaudi, 1985.

Pomar, Anna. *La Cucina Tradizionale Siciliana.* Catania, Sicily: Gruppo Editoriale Brancato, 1988.

Randazzo, Giuseppina. *La Pasticceria Siciliana.* Palermo, Sicily: Gruppo Editoriale Brancato, 1995.

Salomone-Marino, Salvatore. *Customs and Habits of the Sicilian Peasants.* London: Associated University Presses, 1981.

Sciascia, Leonardo. *La Contea di Modica.* Bari, Italy: Leonardo da Vinci Editrice, 1961.

Simeti, Mary Taylor. *On Persephone's Island.* San Francisco: Vintage Books, 1987.

———. *Pomp and Sustenance.* New York: Alfred A. Knopf, 1991.

Stoddard, John L. *Lectures,* vol. 14. Chicago: George L. Shuman, 1905.

Trombetta, Silvia. *Dolci Tradizionali Siciliani.* Catania, Sicily: Gruppo Editoriale Brancato, 1995.

Varvaro, Aurora. *Cucina Eoliana.* Palermo, Sicily: Edizioni Novecento, 1998.

White, K. D. *Roman Farming.* London: Thames and Hudson, 1970.

Wright, Clifford. *Cucina Paradiso.* New York: Simon and Schuster, 1992.

Acknowledgments

I am grateful to many people for accompanying me on this adventure.

Above all, to Judith Regan: thank you for believing in this project and for allowing it to become what it wanted to be. I am inspired by your trust and courage. And to Principessa Lara, *tanti baci!*

To my dear friend and culinary accomplice Monica May, who shared this vision right from the start: thank you for seeing beyond what I saw; for your support and direction; for being bold and fearless and finding all the off-ramps; for your discerning palate, keen insight, and wit; and for holding the light. *Mille grazie, cara amica.*

To Tom Alleman and Linda Lewis: thank you for capturing the essence of Sicily in your exquisite photographs, and for your spirit, patience, and good humor in every situation. It has been an honor.

To Ruta Fox, Amye Dyer, Jeremy Parzen, and Erika Lenkert, who believed I could write and encouraged me to do just that: thank you. And to Cassie Jones for her skillful and patient editorial midwifery: thank you, thank you, thank you.

To Evan Kleiman, who whetted my appetite for Sicily with her food so many years ago, and to Mary Taylor Simeti, who made Sicily come alive for me through her books.

Tante grazie to Bruno Leopardi and Melo Minnella for contributing the exquisite photographs of Sicily's Easter processions.

To Mary Kay Hartley, a fellow Siculophile: thank you for opening doors for me and for sharing my enthusiasm. Thanks also to Silvana Miciletto and Howard Kirschenbaum of Alitalia for making my trips to Sicily smooth, and to Justin Hoy for his expert legal advice. *Molte grazie* to Antonella Cannata for helping me with translations and sharing her childhood memories, and to Connie di Bella for taking me under her wing.

Tanti abbracci to Rosemarie and Stacey Ingenito, with whom I first landed in Palermo, and to Julie Dennis Brothers, for her unbounded optimism. Many thanks to Denise DaVinci and Duane Djck for their keen designers' eye and generosity. To Fayette Hauser: thank you for your infallible artist's sensibility, beautiful props, and good advice.

Much love and gratitude goes to my family: Leah and Gerald Granof; Deborah, Elisa, Ken, Jenny, Judith, Larry, Sydney, and Samantha; Auntie Carol and Uncle Dave; and Nonie, who knew I could do it (and told me so).

And to everyone in Sicily who welcomed me warmly into their shops, their homes, and their lives and shared so generously of their knowledge and talents, especially the Di Bella, Cangemi, Paolino, and Imprescia families: *tante belle cose!*

About the Photographers

LINDA V. LEWIS, the daughter of a Sicilian winemaker, is a fine art and commercial photographer who lives in Los Angeles.

THOMAS MICHAEL ALLEMAN is a photographer who contributes frequently to *People, Time,* and *U.S. News & World Report* and has won the Associated Press's Mark Twain Award for Overall Excellence. He lives in Los Angeles.

MELO MINNELLA was born in Sicily in 1937. A photographer whose career spans more than forty years, he has documented the history and traditions of Sicily in numerous publications throughout the world, including the ten-volume *Storia di Sicilia, Life, Vogue,* and his own book of photographs, *Sicilia Negli Occhi,* published in 1972. He lives in Palermo, Sicily.

Index

MARIS ME:

DITERRA:

NEI

PARS

SICILIA
REGNVM.

Mittell

Meer

MARE